RADICAL COURAGE

HOW ONE MARINE'S SACRIFICE
HELPED CHANGE AMERICA

ERIC ALVA
RETIRED MARINE STAFF SERGEANT
WITH CANDI S. CROSS

DEDICATION

To my husband, Danny, and my parents, Fidelis and Lois.

CONTENTS

ACKNOWLEDGEMENTS

Life is a blessing. I want to begin by acknowledging and thanking my mom and dad for bringing me into this world. I am a product of each of you. I also want to pay homage to my former stepfather, Louis Aguilar. He helped make me the person I am today.

There are so many people in my life that I would like to express my gratitude to. First, my husband, Danny Ingram, for always standing by my side and always supporting me.

Thanks to my good friend, Darrell Parsons, who introduced me to the Human Rights Campaign (HRC). It all happened one night in October 2006, when I decided to send an email to HRC, telling them who I was and asking, "How can I help?" Thank you to Brad Luna for opening and reading that e-mail, which started a journey I did not see coming. I owe so much to HRC and to all the individuals who worked there at the time, for also helping me tell my story. Thank you, Joe Solmonese, for guiding, mentoring, and inspiring me to live my life authentically. I owe a debt of gratitude to everyone at HRC who helped me along my journey.

I could not have been the outspoken speaker today without my agent, a.k.a. "pimp," Dustin Jones formerly of Keppler Speakers and Associates, who marketed me across this country and really helped me get my story out. Working with DJ for thirteen years was a blessing.

Thank you, Mike Kaniuk, for putting up with me as his staff non-commissioned officer; Brian Alaniz for trying to save my life that day I got injured, only to get injured himself. Roger Gomez, my childhood friend since I was twelve years old. Nicholas Hengtes, who gave me the call sign, "Chucky," like the killer doll. Carlos Huerta, Brian Lafferty, and Lavon Peters, whom I served with. All these individuals greatly contributed to helping me tell my story.

A very special "thanks" to my ghostwriter, Candi Cross, for helping me create and share *Radical Courage* in the most vivid way, with radical passion and patience to get it right. Thank you, beautiful friend.

Lastly, thank you to the late Leonard Matlovich, who gave us a face and a voice for so many more to come out. And to All the LGBTQ military men and women, thank you for your service and sacrifices.

PART I
IN SERVICE

CHAPTER 1
WELCOME TO MILITARY CITY, USA

WHAT'S IN A name? Some of us are lucky enough to have a loaded story attached to our name.

I was born a twin in a small, privately owned hospital on the west side of San Antonio. I was given the name "Fidelis Jesse Alva III," after my father and grandfather. I grew up with the nickname, "Pito." According to my beautiful mother, my father would often call me "Papito," a Spanish endearment for *baby boy*. My older sister, Kathy, who was a year and a half when I was born, would call me "Pito" because neither she nor my twin sister could pronounce "Fidelis." Pretty soon, the new name stuck and family members on both sides called me Pito.

In kindergarten, I would even write my name as Pito, only to have the teacher tell me that was not my name. As time went on, I disliked the name, *Fidelis*, and to make matters worse, some teachers refused to roll their tongue around the three syllables and called me "Fidel" or they would spell my name out, pronouncing each letter. The kids in school would call me "Fidel Castro."

By the time I was leaving eighth grade, I started considering different names. Remember back in the 1980s when a nice gentleman would go house to house to sell *Encyclopedia Britannica*. My mom bought a set and that was my foray into name finding. In the set, one went from A-L, then M-Z; the one from A-L consisted of numerous girls' and boys' names to try on. I patiently sat and read through the names and their origin. I finally settled on "Eric."

When I went to high school registration for my freshman year, I filled out "Eric Alva" on all the paperwork. Wow, this felt liberating! I told my friends to start calling me Eric, and before you know it, Fidelis was a thing of the past.

In 1987, when I was about to turn seventeen, my mom asked me if I was serious about changing my name. My mind was made up. She proceeded to hire a lawyer to do the paperwork. I went to court, raised my right hand, and the judge decreed the name "Fidelis Jesse Alva III," to "Eric Fidelis Alva." I was elated. But I did upset my father and grandfather, as I was named after them in honor of their military service. "Fidelis" as in the Marine Corps motto, Semper Fidelis, means "Always faithful." I didn't know where it came from until I joined the Marine Corps and saw the connection. My father had been absent for much of my early life, and no one else bothered to explain the roots of this name. Still, I don't regret changing it. I love the name I have today.

But isn't it astounding how much history a name can carry?

In my experience, it attracts associations, perceptions, and stories that are sometimes unwanted—once collected, they are glued in position. They can't be completely peeled away, and remnants always remain. It wasn't until I started doing media interviews and became an unplanned public figure that I really thought about this notion. I also live in the same city where it all started for my family, the Alvas.

San Antonio is home to one of the largest concentrations of military bases in the United States. It is also home to the Department of Defense's largest medical center at Joint Base San Antonio Fort Sam Houston. Approximately 39,000 students graduate from military training here each year. Roots with the military date back to the first Spanish soldiers who founded the San Antonio de Bexar Presidio in 1718. From its original base at Plaza de Armas in the city's center, to the active military bases scattered throughout the city, you see all things military everywhere. Perhaps we're best known for the U.S. Army Medical Department Museum at Fort Sam Houston and the historic Quadrangle, which is the second oldest military facility in the city. The Fort Sam Houston Museum tells the tale of the evolution of the army in San Antonio, beginning with the establishment of the post in 1845.

And then there are The Missions, a world heritage site, where my husband, Danny, takes every visitor practically before they've finished their first margarita or taco in our fair land! The purpose of The Missions was to convert Native Americans to Christianity.

How profound that gates have established hard lines throughout time. People make gates to keep everyone else out. Neighborhoods are gated communities for that purpose.

San Antonio is also a very colorful and progressive place. Contrasts are striking. In the Fiesta Night Parade, everyone competes with lights on their floats and costumes. In 1891, a group of women decorated horse-drawn carriages, paraded in front of the Alamo, and pelted each other with flower blossoms. The parade was organized to honor the heroes from the battles of the Alamo and San Jacinto and is known as The Battle of Flowers Parade.

I like the name of this parade because my life has been marked by battles of all kinds—except for flowers.

CHAPTER 2
RAMBUNCTIOUS CHILD ON A MISSION

SINCE I WAS born a fraternal twin, my mother always needed help from my father, especially with the feeding and the burping. I must give my mother so much credit for having a one-and-a-half-year-old, and then twins. There were times when we would not fall asleep. My father, being the Hispanic macho man that he was, always insisted on holding me, "his son." That worked for a brief time only because he soon found out I was a squirmer. While my sister fell asleep as soon as my mom rocked her, I would still be wide awake and howling in my dad's arms until my mom took me from him. A sign of things to come.

I was a very rambunctious little boy, although nowadays, some teachers might refer to me as ADHD. My mother says I was a climber and a runner. My mother recalls that every so often, I would knock down the Christmas tree...fully decorated. Once the candy canes on the bottom were gone, she should have plainly moved the top ones down. She never did. I had my eyes set on those swirly sticks, so I would climb on the couch or stand on the chair to get the candy canes, then topple the whole tree over.

Another time that my climbing got me in trouble was when I ascended a fence, which was next to our house. I do not even remember why, but I just liked to climb and jump over things. In the shrub next to the house was a beehive, and I was stung numerous times, causing my face to swell up. By now, you can already guess that I liked getting into things.

My mom was glad when me and Laura started kindergarten and were assigned to the same classroom, but I'm not sure that was a good thing. As rowdy and overactive as I was, Laura was sweet and quiet.

One day in class, my teacher was running copies on an old copy machine called a mimeograph, which used mass-market purple or blue ink that easily smudged. When the teacher stepped out for few minutes, I saw the opportunity to get into the waste basket and retrieve the blue copy paper. I started passing it to the other kids in the classroom, including Laura. I smeared the blue ink all over my face and arms, and so did the other kids. Let's just say, when the teacher returned, she was livid. She sent poor Laura home with me, along with a note. After arriving home, my mother was without words and already knew who the instigator in this evil ploy was. She instructed us to stand in the living room and wait for our father to get home. Lucky for us, he seemed amused actually.

The moral of these childhood antics is that I simply could not sit still. Ever.

In the fourth grade, I was on the safety patrol in charge of the crosswalks. I would have to get to school early to put the sign out for the cars to stop for the kids. By fifth grade, I was a sergeant—I really thought I was a police officer! Ambition can be seeded quite early.

I had a paper route at the age of eight and even operated on weekends. I learned the importance of hard work, discipline, and scheduling, but I also learned obstacles and setbacks. I never saw achievement as something that came easy or to be taken for granted. Proving this on my paper route, I once fell out of the car my mother was driving and hit my head on the asphalt. I was sitting on the right side of the passenger seat and went to grab my papers on the left. My mom took a sharp turn, and I flew out the window weightless and incidental in that moment. All these years later, I can still feel the sensation of my head hitting the road.

One time, my mom got me so upset that I threw her car keys on top of the roof. I thought nothing of her frustration. When she asked why I did it, my simple answer was that there is a negative response when you don't get your way. This time, it was just car keys that were retrievable with a bit of effort. In another instance of not getting my way, I stuck a hose in the car exhaust, stalling it. Perhaps that was more audacious.

My behavior might have been aggressive sometimes, and I liked to push my physical abilities to the limit. However, I recoiled from any kind of violence. I didn't like to see anyone hurt.

Our father taught me and Laura how to box one another with professional boxing gloves. I refused to hit Laura and would break down crying when he instructed me to do so.

When I heard about some schools in the South reinstating corporal punishment, my body had a physical reaction. I cringe thinking of how many times I got paddled at home. The very sight of a violent act coming brought on nausea. In those times, I would make myself move more. It was as if my own motions would thwart violence of any kind if it were in my peripheral.

I have always been an active person. I used to play Little League baseball, but I royally sucked at it. I wanted to play football, but I was too small in stature. Finally, I found power in running. I started to run track in eighth grade and became a solid runner, yet it didn't crush the pent-up energy within. As one would expect, being the smallest boy didn't score me any free passes with the bullies. My friend, Roger Gomez, recalls that he watched me beat the hell out of one of these bullies. I didn't want to fight, but I learned that sticking up for myself—and others—would rarely be done in a comfort zone.

CHAPTER 3
A FAMILY'S WAR WOUNDS

DO YOU KNOW anyone who served in the Vietnam War? I mean *really* know someone? For me, this person is my father, and his time in combat greatly affected him. We need only consider that post-traumatic stress disorder (PTSD) was first recognized as a mental health condition in 1980, just five years after the end of the Vietnam War. For hundreds of years, these symptoms have been described under different names in soldiers from many wars. However, Vietnam veterans with these symptoms were the first to have the term, *post-traumatic stress disorder* (PTSD) applied to them.

My father was raised in a clean, comfortable home in the better part of the west side, in a nice neighborhood called Loma Park. He was what was called an "Army brat." His father served in the army for twenty years before retiring, having fought in WWII and Korea. The neighborhood was fairly new, the houses were recently built. Here, my father made lifelong friends. He has happy memories of growing up there.

My mother was born fourth in a family that would eventually consist of ten children; four boys and six girls. Needless to say, she was raised on a much lower economic level than my father. Her father also served in the army during WWII.

Both of my parents attended Edgewood High School, with my father graduating in 1966, and my mother in 1968. Was it fate or was it serendipity that brought them together on a rainy day while both attending high school? She a freshman and he a senior. She loved his sense of humor and easygoing manner. They were a couple through high school until Vietnam, and the military draft came into the picture. My father volunteered for the army in 1967, and as most Hispanic young men out of high school and not attending college, wound up in Vietnam at the age of eighteen. I heard my mother say the young man she loved had boarded a plane in San Antonio bound for Vietnam and never returned. A stranger returned in his place. There were no physical wounds when he returned home, but she immediately noticed a change. He returned a sullen, humorless man. He preferred not to be around crowds and seemed to be constantly vigilant.

They were married in 1968, two weeks before my mother graduated from high school. My mother told me that a week into their marriage, she felt a state of panic and asked herself, "What did I do? I married a crazy person." The man she had hoped to show off at graduation functions was a reluctant date. He was miserable at prom and with other high school kids. He was no longer a kid. He had returned a man, but not the same man she loved. My dad had already begun developing a drinking problem. He was often angry because he wasn't old enough to buy beer at age twenty but had been old enough to have a weapon shoved in his hands and sent to war at age eighteen.

The *San Antonio Report*, "nonprofit journalism for an informed community," reported that Bexar County lost 300 men in the Vietnam War. According to the National Archives report on U.S. Fatal Casualties of the Vietnam War, fifty-five of them were from Edgewood Independent School District, with two high schools, and most of them Hispanic. According to the Edgewood District Veterans chapter, ten were part of Edgewood High School's class of '67, which had 460 seniors, 235 of whom were male. The veteran group's historian, Mario Longoria, said "the school district had one of the highest fatal casualty numbers in the country."

My parents were married for fourteen years, eventually ending up in a bitter divorce. Perhaps the cruelest aspect of the war was the treatment of the returning soldiers. Unlike the hero status given to the returning soldiers from World War II, the soldiers that served in Vietnam were often met at the airport by protesters calling them names such as "baby killers," "psychos," "drug addicts," and worse. All of this effected not only the soldiers, but also, their families. My father would not talk to his wife about what he had experienced, or the TET offensive, the Vietnamese New Year. On January 30, 1968, North Vietnamese and Viet Cong troops launched an all-out attack against the South Vietnamese and United States targets. This became a major turning point in the Vietnam War.

After being honorably discharged, my dad returned to his job at Swearingen Aircraft as a sheet metal mechanic at the rate of $2.10 an hour; minimum wage at the time was $1.25. My older sister, Katherine, was born a year and a half later followed by my twin sister, Laura, and me another year and a half after. By this time, most of the old neighborhood lifelong friends returned home. A few did not. One that grew up on the same street as my dad did not make it home, and another was critically wounded. All were proud to be home after having served their country. Most of these guys came home with problems. Getting together to drink and talk about Vietnam became the thing to do. In the beginning, my mom blamed his friends for his drinking. She then blamed the US government and the stress in Vietnam. And finally, she blamed the US Army for making available the beer and for their leniency on pot. He told her how pallets of beer would be flown in, making it always available. Fourteen years later after the drinking began to get worse, she could only blame him.

Approximately 38% of Vietnam veteran marriages failed within six months of the veterans' return from Southeast Asia. My parents were part of the overall divorce group where the rate among Vietnam veterans was significantly higher than for the general population, and for veterans with PTSD the rates were even higher. This marriage never stood a chance. After the divorce, my mother remarried, and my father continued to drink until he eventually joined AA.

My mom often tells me she sees a lot of my dad in me, not only in looks, but also, in character. She does not tell me what traits she sees, but I can assume. She tells me my father was a man of principles before he went to Vietnam, but he returned an alcoholic. He hurt himself and his family without realizing how badly. I have to look inside myself at times. Am I becoming what my dad once was? Am I becoming an alcoholic? How badly do I need a drink in order to face everyday life and stress? And most importantly, am I beginning to mistreat the people closest to me, people that I'm supposed to love and protect? Are they making excuses for me like my mom did for my dad because she loved him so?

I know I changed after my experiences in Somalia and being injured in Iraq. The main question I must ask myself is, "Do I have the courage and the strength of heart to do what my dad did and seek help?"

I didn't speak to my dad for almost thirteen years after he and my mom divorced. As I got older, I got angrier. I replaced my real father with my stepfather. My stepfather was kind and accepted us as his own. He already had two boys of his own around the same age as us. They would stay with us on and off. I had an extremely hard time getting along with the oldest. In hindsight, I can see how they must have felt: pushed aside for three other children and a stepmom. Eventually this marriage broke up, too.

The reason for the earlier word, *serendipity*, is because after my mother's second marriage broke up, she and my father came back together as parents of three kids and grandparents of two little girls. They rekindled the same love and affection of their earlier pre-Vietnam days. The difference being a newly discovered friendship and understanding. I am very proud of my parents; my dad is still in AA with twenty-nine years of sobriety. He has made amends to us, his children, and I'm sure to my mom. My mom says she never stopped loving my father. She forgave him many years before. After a bout with breast cancer, and my father by her side taking care of her, she retired from teaching. They are both now enjoying retirement, life, and each other. My dad is a regular golfer and loves kayaking, and my mom spends time in her garden and caring for her great-grandson who is now the light of her life. She also spends time traveling with her sisters.

Their enjoyment of life together still amazes me, as I think back to rough times when we were all separated and on the edge.

CHAPTER 4
FAITHFUL

I N HIGH SCHOOL, needing somewhere else to project my voice other than home, I ran for class president and student council. I passed out candy to everyone to vote for me. My ploy worked, and I realized that I liked the power in being a leader and making a difference. What difference did I truly make in high school? I'm not sure I thought about it much, but I made it a point to be in class on time and be friendly to everyone, including my teachers.

When my friend, Hector, made it into the U.S. Marine Corps, I attended his graduation. We both shared this aspiration to serve our country.

My mom did not want me to go into the military. She was so fearful that I would get hurt or be deployed like my father one day—or turn out like him if I ever saw combat. I was still working at the restaurant after high school graduation. I wanted to be independent. I wanted to start my own life. When I enlisted, she just couldn't believe it. I was turning nineteen. It was the best decision of my life other than marrying my husband, Danny! Serving my country helped me become the person I am today.

I came home with the folder of signed paperwork, joining the military and I had a U.S. Marine Corps T-shirt on. Livid, my mother yelled, "Take that off!" She couldn't talk me out of going, however.

I used to have epilepsy as a kid. I would have seizures quite a bit, as did my twin sister. She grew out of them before me. I grew out of my epilepsy by the time I was sixteen years old. I didn't have this as an adult. I was truthful about it when I first tried to enlist. They sent me to the army doctors for a plethora of tests. I was cleared and was about to enlist, on the condition of gaining twelve pounds. I looked like I was ten years old trying to get into the Marine Corps!

Because of my small physique, some of the recruiters looked at me like I was out of my mind.

I had started the enlistment process in fall of 1989 and got cleared to enlist in June of 1990. I had to wait nine more months because of my assigned job not being open yet.

On March 4, 1991, the day came for me to head to boot-camp. I was one of five men leaving from the San Antonio area. A twenty-nine-year-old recruit was put in charge of "looking out for me" once I got assigned to Marine Corps Recruit Depot (MCRD), San Diego, Calif. After arriving at MCRD, we were told to get off the bus and get on the infamous "yellow footprints." We had a saying, "asshole to belly buttons." I would be crammed in these lines of men, all who were taller than me, and I had my nose to their backs. I was among the shortest—if not the shortest—recruit at 5'1." I stood out like a sore thumb.

On my first day in line, the drill sergeant stopped in my direction, shouting, "What the fuck is this?" He literally grabbed me out of line and told me to put my arms out and lock my elbows. He picked me up and said, "My shit weighs more than this."

I didn't know how to react after he dropped me. I squeezed back in line with the other recruits. This was thirty minutes after standing on those yellow footprints. Then I got the comments:

"Did you sneak in here?"

"Do your parents know where you are?"

"Did you run away from home?"

It was nonstop harassment.

I had promised my mother that when I joined the military that we would never be in another war, like I could predict that. Well, "Never say never."

By December 1992, a year and half after joining the United States Marine Corps, I was sent to Somalia for Operation Restore

Hope, the day after my twenty-second birthday. I was there for a couple of months in a very short deployment. That place was awful. No central government reemerged to take the place of the overthrown government, and the United States closed its embassy that same year, although the two countries never broke off diplomatic relations. The country descended into chaos, and a humanitarian crisis of staggering proportions began to unfold.

The United Nations attempted to address the crisis with United Nations Operation in Somalia (UNOSOM) to provide humanitarian assistance, created by the United Nations Security Council via Resolution 751 in April 1992. The United States sent food aid via Operation Provide Comfort starting in August 1992.

Intense fighting between the warlords impeded the delivery of aid to those who needed it most, and so the United Nations contemplated stronger action.

I remember the day before I was scheduled to leave the country and return to the United States, I volunteered for a security detail. We were returning some weapons back to the port. During our three-vehicle convoy in which I was on the end vehicle, we stopped because the lead vehicle had come to a halt as Somali nationals blocked the streets. Our vehicle was quickly surrounded by Somali nationals. They started to swarm the vehicle. They were shouting at us and throwing rocks and objects. They came up to the driver and snatched his sunglasses off. He turned off the vehicle and started chasing the young kids who did that. Before I knew it, the Somali nationals were trying to take the vehicle. I had my M-16 loaded and ready to fire, but I couldn't. Instead, I grabbed a pipe in the back of the Humvee, started to swing it and hit some of the people. Eventually the driver came back and started the vehicle, and we took off. We were instructed only to fire as a "last resort." This was all before "Black Hawk Down."

I often wonder what that day might have turned out to be if we didn't get away. Would I still be here today?

CHAPTER 5
RISING AND RUNNING

AFTER RETURNING HOME from Somalia, I met a new Marine in our unit who had arrived while I was overseas. He didn't speak much, and I thought he was too quiet. I eventually befriended him, and he started to talk to me more. He was one rank below me and technically, we were not supposed to "socialize" because I was a non-commissioned officer. Well, aside from the rules and regulations, we did start hanging out together. So much that we formed a relationship. He was my first relationship with someone of the same sex. He was kind and four years younger than me. This was 1993 when the newly elected commander-in-chief was now promising the country he would "allow" lesbian, gay, bisexual, and transgender individuals to serve openly in the United States Armed Forces. As time went on, I had this paranoid feeling that other Marines noticed that the two of us were more than just friends. I knew I loved being overseas and I knew I had to separate the both of us before we were found out and punished by law.

I wanted to see more of the world, so in the summer of 1994, I left him behind in Twentynine Palms, California—I put in the paperwork for me to be sent overseas again, this time to Okinawa. (We recently reconnected, and he is happily married to his wife, and they have a child.)

While in Okinawa, I became a huge runner. I ran my ass off. I started running marathons in 1995. My personal record (PR) was 3:10 in the Marine Corps Marathon, and I was in the top 600 out of 19,000 estimated runners. And to be honest, I had picked up speed in Okinawa primarily to suppress sexual urges! At one time, I wondered if the military would "make me straight." Then of course, good-looking, muscular men surrounded me. I had to shut off my feelings from time to time.

While stationed in Okinawa, most Marines used to go to Whisper Alley, a dark place where you could unzip your pants for oral sex. They didn't care whose face was behind those lips. Instead of Whisper Alley, I would go running around the perimeter of the base, eight miles. Then I would go get a pizza or hamburger and bring it back to my room and settle in with a movie. My roommate was always out either at the club in the village or Whisper Alley during that time. The next morning, I would run again. People called me "The Running Fool."

Kristin Beck said of this kind of experience in her book, *Warrior Princess*, "burn it out," "run it out," "work it out." Known as "Lady Valor" because of her fearlessness in combat, Kristin had served over twenty years in the Special Operations Forces. She is the recipient of more than fifty distinguished ribbons and metals, including the Bronze Star and Purple Heart. Her heroic journey consists of thirteen deployments, seven combat deployments, and several tours with the counter-terrorism Naval Special Warfare Development Group. In 2013, Kristin began the courageous transition from male to female. I don't know what her urges were, but mine had always been connected to other males.

In the military, at least when I served, you were either going to become a PT freak, always working out and running, a Bible thumper, who would be in prayer groups constantly, or a drunk. I preferred to be the running fool.

In June of 1995, Father's Day, I was in Okinawa. I didn't have a car and couldn't do much on the island. The USO was pretty crowded that day, with everyone getting out calling cards to phone their fathers. I hesitated. Then I went to the counter and asked for a card. I called my sister for my dad's number. I got in the phone booth, closed the door, and called him.

He picked up and I said, "Happy Father's Day, Dad, it's Eric."

He started to cry. I had not seen my father in thirteen years. He couldn't speak for a while. Then his first words were, "I'm sorry. I'm sorry. I'm sorry." His voice cracked into little pieces, gasping with sorrow. I didn't reply.

My sister had informed him I was in the Marine Corps and in Japan, so he knew about a fraction of my life—namely, that I had followed in his and his father's combat boots despite my mother's horror.

I was in Japan for a year, and it was time to return to Texas. I was given a thirty-day leave pass to visit home. My dad asked if he could come to the airport to meet me. By this time, I had moved on from some of my fury over what he had done to my childhood, so I agreed. But there was a twist. My mother, who had not seen him for years, alongside my stepfather, showed up. I was turning twenty-five that year. The three of them made small talk and were civil. My dad looked exceptionally aged. He was the perfect display of what so much alcohol can do to your insides and appearance. I tried not to show how astonished I was.

While at home, my twin sister, Laura, had informed me that Mom "knew." "Knew what?" I asked. She said that our mother had found a letter mentioning that me and my first love had broken up while I was in Japan and that she now knew I was gay even though I had not formally informed her. Despite being on a thirty-day pass of leave, I did not stay at home long because I knew I was in trouble with my mother. Even at twenty-four years old, she scared me, and I didn't want to disappoint her.

For my next duty, I got stationed in California once again. I didn't want to go home that Christmas because I knew my mom had discovered the truth about me.

On January 17, 1996, my mother called the barracks, wanting to speak to me. She asked why I didn't come home and why I had not called to let them know how I was doing. It was there on that pay phone, I shouted, "You know why!" Then I pressured her over and over to just tell me the truth of what she knew. She started crying.

"Say it! Say it! Say that your son is a faggot!" I pressed.

She cried, "Stop it, Eric. Stop it!"

Interestingly, my mother never came off as a homophobe. Neither of my parents had. But again, she had a delusional definition of "family," and this may have had something to do with the religious order that older generations in our family identified with. We would faithfully go to Catholic church on Sundays. When I told my grandmother, Mom exploded. I don't even think her response was out of shame, as it was one of molded ideas in her of how she wanted me to be. I've never been a parent, and I certainly did not follow the family's playbook, which instructed me to pass on the family name.

The Marines developed a different connotation around my name. When they saw me coming, they would jump off the sidewalk and stand there firmly, giving me a greeting. One officer would not show me any respect at all; in fact, he completely ignored me. It's like he refused to acknowledge authority, and I'm not even sure why he was there in the first place. However, several of my fellow Marines would become lifelong friends with decorated careers. Ultimately, they would also see me in living hell.

Carlos Huerta joined the Marine Corps in 2000 and went through the Officer Candidate School. By this time, I ran the supply unit for 3d Battalion, 7 Marines. On September 12, 2001, he was a new officer and had been in California for less than two months with an exceptional senior staff in an upstanding platoon before being named second lieutenant and representing the platoon. When he made it to the infantry that summer, I had just come back from Okinawa. His motor transport platoon had been mixed up a little bit, so he had newbies coming in. I was a staff sergeant, and the unit Carlos came from included E7 and E6 individuals. Several of us were in a staff meeting together before we actually met.

Carlos paints a portrait of me in those formative years: "One of my staff sergeants had taken me to the staff meeting, indicating that 'Alva's here' and if you say something stupid, he will call you on it! Right out the gate, I saw someone who had the same level of responsibilities, the same actions. He caught my attention because I was new doing something for the platoon and he was seasoned. Eric would make comments to me like, 'Your staffing senior should be doing this…doing that,' so from there, we made a professional friendship. He was giving me good information and he helped me out. His specialty was supply chain and logistics. We leaned on Eric's group for supplies and when they tried to push their weight around, Eric would take control. He was intimidating in that he knew his shit, his field, and he didn't want others wasting time. As a Marine, he set the example. If you were supposed to do something, he always did it without question. Other people looked for loopholes, but he was very disciplined. It was hard to find someone who did everything correctly. You could see that Eric was on the path to be a sergeant major. As an E6, he carried himself almost as an E8 to become an E9.

"Everyone makes mistakes and I'm sure Alva had some of his own, but you wouldn't know it. He never showed it. He is somebody who is there for you. He represented the Marine Corps very well. He set the example. He didn't take slack or second place from anybody. He made sure he was in charge in his area and that others followed the rules. I saw him call other Marines out. And he's not that tall! I'm 6"1' and I remember him grabbing another Marine and pulling him down, putting his finger in his face and not batting an eye. We would drink coffee in the morning, and he took the time to explain some stuff to me as a mentor in his desire to make me look good because it made the Marine Corps look good."

I met Brian Lafferty in January of 2001 after I gave my no-nonsense, rather dry speech about being "by the book" and "not to ask me to cut corners or to expect my supplies division to cut corners to compensate for other people's mistakes." Soon after our friendly intro, we got into a converted 747 together, entirely coach, no business or first class. At the front of the plane, where the nose is, getting narrow, there are fewer seats. Brian and the motor transport chief were both around 190 pounds. They were considerably larger than me, but I ran fifty miles a week and I knew that I epitomized a fit Marine, one not to be taken lightly. They called me a "tiny dude" anyway.

I sat in between Brian and the motor transport chief in the center aisle for what was a fifteen-hour plane ride to Okinawa, and that is how we got to know each other. Low and behold, by the time that horrendous flight ended, we knew quite a lot about each other.

In Okinawa, Brian had overseen computers and communications equipment. We worked closely together, and our friendship evolved. That deployment to Okinawa could be characterized by drinking on Friday nights, throwing darts in the staff club, and playing racquetball. As our next deployment together would be to Iraq, I'm not sure there could be a greater contrast between the two assignments.

About six months after returning home from Okinawa as staff non-commissioned officer in charge (meaning, the senior enlisted to our $9 million supply section), my supply officer at the time was leaving the unit and I was due to receive a new OIC (officer in charge). I was turning thirty-one that year, and Mike Kaniuk was scheduled to arrive soon. Lieutenant Carlos Huerta brought him into my office. I swear, I thought he was seventeen years old. He was so young. He had his hands behind his back and when we shook hands, his hands were a little sweaty. He may have been nervous about meeting me.

Here I am about to pass eleven years in the Marine Corps, and I think Mike had only been in for less than two. My job was to be his "chief of staff," advise and guide him while following his orders because he oversaw the supply section for a battalion of 900+ male Marines. Mike was the sole person responsible for the unit's bank account worth millions. My job was to protect him and not let people take advantage of him. Or at least that's how I felt. If it was Mike or anyone else in that role, I was going to help them. Our supply section was part of a "company," along with seven other sections like admin, motor transport, the cooks, the navy corpsman (our combat medics), communications, and a few others. I explain this because in each "section," there was another SNCOIC (staff non-commissioned officer in charge), just like me, paired up with an OIC (officer in charge) like Mike.

When Lavon Peters joined the unit, I was grateful I got a hard-charging Marine. He was really "good to go," as we say. Lavon and I bonded right away because he recognized that I was squared away like him, fit, and I took my job very seriously. We hung out together sometimes. When we got deployed, Lavon arrived in the Middle East a few weeks after I did. But before deployment, I think I was mostly rough on Lavon. I wanted almost perfection before deployment, so I yelled at him a lot. He took it with a grain of salt, and he always made me proud.

Lavon recalls, "I remember standing there waiting for my new supervisor and I saw this little gentleman come around a corner. His demeanor was very serious. I was like, 'oh God! What have I gotten into?' Even though Eric was very serious, I loved working with him, and I've always gone to him for leadership advice. He always stood his ground. He always stood up for the Marines who worked with him. He always stood by his morals. Regardless of if it wasn't the most popular decision, he stood by what was right for the institution."

In the run up to being deployed to the Middle East, Lavon had been there on different deployments before, including a Mediterranean tour. He would be the one to see me sleeping at the station sometimes in the middle of the night or early in the morning. I worked nonstop.

As a Navy Corpsmen, Brian Alaniz assisted Navy physicians with providing medical treatment for sailors and Marines. He had completed special training in combat medics and weapons. As such, while stationed with the Marines, Brian was directly responsible for seeing Marines when they were sick or injured.

He explains, "We take their temperature, blood pressure, respirations per minute. We do the write-ups in their medical folders and then have to present our case to the medical officer. We go out and PT with the Marines. During combat operation, a Navy corpsman is the first to treat a wounded Marine or sailor on the front lines before they are medevacked to be seen by a medical officer. Wherever the Marines go, the Navy corpsman goes."

He remembers being taken aback by my size, particularly when I was yelling (as if physical stature dictates tone of voice). We completed a ten-mile hike in the desert of Kuwait. We were about halfway done, and Brian started to fall behind a little. I helped him catch up with the rest of the group. In turn, later that day, Brian treated me for a scratched cornea. We talked and found out we were both from Texas and both of us promised our parents we would be back in one piece.

CHAPTER 6
AMERICA'S NEW, UNCERTAIN ORDER

MIKE KANIUK HAD only been in Kuwait for about two months when we received the big announcement in a staff meeting: It was time to go to Iraq with the aim of finding Iraqi weapons of mass destruction (WMD) and ending the dictatorial rule of Saddam Hussein.

I was sitting behind Mike as the commander started up the conversation with, "Gentlemen, we're going to war." He looked back at me, and I just nodded my head in acknowledgement as if to say, *we'll get through this together. I'll help you along, young lieutenant.*

I didn't get a chance to chew on the gravity of this deployment before being assigned to the advancement team, which meant that I would be going in a couple of months prior to the main cavalcade. We had to obtain gear from maritime ships. I led the team to pull the equipment off the ship, test it and take receipt of it so we could use it for our battalion. Mike came two to three weeks later with the main body of the battalion.

"Half of what I felt was fear of the unknown; the other half, being prepared," said Mike. "We had prepared for it. We did a lot of training, coupled with being there with those guys I was leading. Just having your friends there made it easier, but I had a little bit of nervousness in what was going down."

Mike's professional goal had been to obtain a sociology degree with criminal justice options in order to get into federal law enforcement. A buddy had talked him into joining the Marines, going so far as taking him to his physical, and signing him up.

Before being deployed to the Middle East, in the summer of 2002, we were starting to prepare the whole unit for months of urban training for encountering citizens in metropolitan areas. What we didn't know in that period of summer training was that we were training for *Iraq*. Mike had a great deal of pressure on him. People were always asking him for things and even favors. He had to learn how to do tasks on his own, and I saw him grow exponentially. As time went on and training taxed us all, I became a thorn in Mike's ass—not because I wanted to, but we were preparing for war and everyone was under a lot of stress, including me.

I flew my mother out to California to see me before leaving for the Middle East. During the four days she was staying with me, I only saw her for a few hours each day because I had to work so much. With 9/11 having occurred in the last year, we couldn't see off family members at the airport gates any longer. Think about that for a moment. Anyone used to be able to clear security in most airports even if they weren't flying. Interestingly, some airlines do issue you a special access gate pass for military passenger family members…like the good, old days!

In any case, when I took my mom to the Palm Springs International Airport, she did not want to let me go. She kept pleading, "Don't go…I don't feel good about this. Please, Eric… *don't go.*" Her whole energy reeked of sadness as if foreshadowing deep mourning. I cried on the way back to my base. I broke my mother's heart.

Brian Alaniz was doubtful that we would even go into Iraq since the corpsmen maintained a calendar and they all had picked a day when they thought we were going to get sent back home. When they finally got the orders to go into Iraq, Brian and the others had come off a night exercise and had been asleep for about two hours. Some thought it was a joke. Brian and I knew the very mention of "combat" was not a laughing matter. Ultimately, the joke would be on us.

He said, "I thought, why are we going in? Is this just a stunt by the President so he doesn't seem weak? Is the reason the President

Radical Courage

has given a good enough reason to start a war? Then on the other hand, we heard the things that Saddam Hussein had done to his own people while in power and thought this guy needed to be taken out of power for being like Hitler. When we finally crossed the border into Iraq, I could see that the people there were coming out to the streets and waving and smiling. It made me feel like we were doing the right thing."

On January 15, 2003, I was among the first wave of about 1,000 people sent to Kuwait. I was with thirty or forty people from my unit of all different specialties, from operations, supply, and medical. Kuwait is a booming city now with a gleaming skyline and impressive theatre scene even, but that had not been my experience of the place.

In our bus, the windows were covered by thick curtains so we couldn't see out. It had a musty smell. We were not on asphalt. When it finally stopped, they opened the door and we all got off the bus. It was complete darkness. The only light we had was from headlights. As soon as the driver left, we could barely see anything in front of us. We had no tent. Each one of us had gear but supplies that were required to set up camp had not arrived. It appeared that we would be there for at least two days.

On the second day, it started to rain. Then it poured. This marked my twelve-year stint in the Marine Corps, and I was thirty-two years old. All I remember is waking up that morning in a poncho liner after the rain stopped and thinking, why the hell do I keep doing this shit? We were all using the bathroom like cats in a litter box, digging holes in the sand, and just going! I couldn't fathom anything more miserable at the time.

CHAPTER 7
MY SHOCK AND AWE

ON THE DAY my life would change so drastically, I remember shaking Mike Kaniuk's hand, wishing him well on our deployment and thinking how far he had come. I was so very proud of him.

In the meantime, Brian Lafferty had been conducting rigorous convoy drills because he was on convoy operations for days and days and days heading up into Iraq. He would do his regular job during the day and then at night, perform convoy exercises. Receiving the signal to move, Brian had been awake for at least two days. He was utterly exhausted before crossing into Iraq.

The established route was the desert to the west side of the main highway, onto the highway once cleared and the drive right into Iraq, through the unit checkpoint, crossing into Kuwait. That night, they experienced some weird friendly fire incident in which one of our helicopters fired on one of the tanks.

War became real.

Neither Brian nor most Marines with him had been through anything like that. Explosions bloomed in the distance. The sky lit up. It was really strange.

The next day, the sun came up and Brian's convoy started moving. He remembers that day vividly: "The action was to move a little bit and wait hours. Move more and wait hours. We finally crossed into Iraq and went into a border town, which was not where we were supposed to stop. We shot through this town and were going into the next town further to the north. Our line consisted of what they call the 'logistics train', which was all the supplies, fuels, and maintenance of approximately one hundred Humvees and bigger trucks, some with trailers; some without.

They had picked this area for us to pause in. It's a big open space. Inside was a dilapidated Iraqi artillery position—a headquarters bunker and two or three Iraqi artillery pieces that were for show. I don't think they would have worked. We were supposed to go in there and just wait until the infantry reign went into the town to do their job and then we were going to join them and plan the next evolution of the attack into Iraq.

"We rolled into this place, and it was just littered with bomblets, a type of bomb that United States employs. It bursts in the air into a bunch of small grenades, and they usually explode when they hit the ground because they have little triggers on them. The problem is they don't all explode. We pulled in there anyway. For most of us, this was our first time to the rodeo. There was maybe one or two people who had seen actual combat in 1991. The young Marines were giddy with excitement. They had been in these Humvees for hours and hours and hours. They got out to explore the area, looking in the bunkers. I walked around, trying to get them all to go back to the Humvees and stay put. They went back. No one got hurt. Then everything was calm."

Carlos, who had arrived in Iraq with me, was in the convoy behind mine. We traveled with a separation of a mile or 500 yards. We were traveling at night. It's "declassified" now, but the mission was to race to Baghdad as fast as you can and bypass all the cities. The United States hadn't gone into real conflict since the Gulf War, a four-day ground war. At the time, you had the Army and Marines. It was a common theory that fifteen years later, enter Iraqi Freedom, and the U.S. armed forces were competing for bragging rights to who would arrive first.

Carlos remembers asking and he was told to go around the cities, that there would be no reason to get into conflict with them. As soon as we crossed the border, the mission changed to Basra. All the excitement to get there deflated quickly. The Army was now going to Baghdad and the Marines, Al Basra, toward Persian Gulf.

We went to this one position just outside of Basra and Alpha Command had been up most of the night. They pulled away a certain distance into an empty lot. Iraqis were there and we pushed them out of this open space that spanned the size of two football fields. We made a big circle, cleared it out, and then turned around. It got quiet. We had been up all night. People were tired and we didn't have all the info about the rest of the country. We started to get out of the vehicles to plan. Carlos walked back to the vehicles and saw all these things on the ground.

Someone said, "Watch out for these things. We don't know what they are. I'm telling everyone."

Maybe one hour went by.

Carlos got into the Humvee and drove to the Alpha Command. We could not have been there more than fifteen minutes. In fact, Carlos took off his boots to rub his feet.

He had taken off one boot and the captain came up and said, "We need to get back. Someone was injured."

Carlos was flabbergasted. "Where? In our position? We were just there!" Had the Iraqis returned? We had superior firepower. No way. Lavon shared the same feeling of shock and exhaustion, as there had been a horrible sandstorm the day before, which seemed a little ominous to Lavon. Lavon got out of the Humvee from the back. He stood there scanning his surroundings. What happened next would alter our understanding of war.

"Before we got there, we would pull over to the side of the road. Eric was fearless. He would get out and make sure the area was clear. Everyone else was hesitant, looking at him like he didn't have any fear. He didn't mind being the first one out of the vehicle and making sure things were okay. On this particular day, when he got out, we were talking, and I had a round in the chamber. I was trying to get it out because there was so much sand. Eric doesn't know this part [until now]—he stepped on the landmine, and I thought my weapon shot him! I was in shock. Then I realized as someone else was running over toward us, as they stepped on a landmine. I remember seeing pieces of him just lying around. He was looking up at me. Someone applied a tourniquet. I was telling him that he would be okay…but I didn't know if he was going to make it."

Brian Lafferty heard the explosion and saw people running. He got on the radio and started talking to our higher headquarters because they needed to know what was going on. It was obvious a helicopter would be needed to retrieve this casualty, or casualties, because at the time, Brian didn't know who or how many.

The medical guys started setting up. They were part of the logistics train and broke out their equipment, such as sawhorses that you put stretchers on. The setup becomes a hospital bed. Big cases that have all the stuff you would see in emergency rooms. They popped a couple open to receive casualties. Right there where they were, another explosion rocked the sky and ground. A second man was critically wounded. Five people caught shrapnel from that explosion.

The helicopters buzzed overhead.

Someone said, "Alva won't stop screaming."

Brian thought, *that is just like Eric—someone got blown up and Eric can't take it.* "He will scream his head off instead of solving the problem."

The guy that Brian said this to replied, "He's the one that's hurt!"

Nicholas Hengtes was the supervisor for his section (the cooks). Nick and I had a solid bond. I used to hang out with him after hours at the enlisted club with other people. We had both done the six-month deployment to Okinawa and even came home together in July of 2001, a month before the whole unit returned in August 2001. Well, after 9/11, everything also changed for Nick, as he got enmeshed in training during the year of 2002 and deployed with me to the Middle East.

By this time, Nick oversaw the logistics department, so he became my supervisor once promoted to master sergeant. I was on Nick's convoy. Nick was with me when the land pulverized me. I never saw his face hovering over me. Within seconds, the medical doctor and medics were treating me. I understand that some people running toward me already thought I was dead because the blast had been so powerful. Nick held out hope. We had a great working relationship even though he had nicknamed me "Chuckie" (as in the killer doll from the movies)!

The least I could do was chuckle for being called well, Chuckie, from time to time. I know that it wasn't always easy to work with "Staff Sergeant Alva," and not because I was a tyrant, but because I worked hard and tried to make every task and situation perfect. Goals were gains. Loss was for losers.

When Carlos headed back to position, someone ran up to him and shouted, "Alva got hit! ...And another one got hit!"

All this stuff was racing through his head. How? They didn't explain it. That's when he learned those little parachutes were landmines, explosive devices designed to kill people and destroy vehicles. Shrapnel had hit seven or eight people. Carlos turned around, wondering where I was. The whole area was quiet. The helicopter had come in and lifted me off. They evacuated me right away. From when I last talked to him, maybe only thirty minutes had passed. We had been talking for five or ten minutes next to my Humvee, where this happened.

At this point, Brian Lafferty had a hard time computing the gruesome images in front of him. As the helicopter lifted, another Marine's foot was injured, and they were going to try to evacuate him by Humvee ambulance. They drove off but then they came back. One of Brian's Marines, Steven, was also injured, and shrapnel hit his chief's wedding band. It bent the ring into his finger and probably saved him from losing the finger.

Brian chokes up when he thinks about that day. "We had a

bulldozer to plow through these bomblets and create a clear path for everyone to drive out. As they were doing this, sometimes the bulldozer's blade would set them off. The blade protected the operator, but while clearing the lanes for us to escape, right near Eric's Humvee, they found landmines. I don't think we will ever know for sure whether he stepped on a landmine or whether he kicked a bomblet. The truth is, we never should have gone into that position. I know people that made those decisions to go in there. It weighs heavily on them. The logistics officer in charge of what we were doing ultimately put us in there. That field, one of the infantry companies swept through that area in armored vehicles; they should have warned us that area was unsafe and made the call for us not to go in there. They planned for a month or six weeks what we would do on this first day, but I'm not sure they could deviate from the plan. I don't think there was any way we weren't going in there. It took us hours to get out of there, with all these vehicles on the same path. For five tanks, you get like twenty vehicles to support them—mechanics and fluids, fuel. For when we got out of there, what we ended up doing is parking on the side of the road. If we had done that from the get-go...."

Mike Kaniuk was with the commanding officer and heard about the explosions on the radio. "I said, I hope it's not Alva. Two reasons: He was my right-hand man, and I didn't want to see him hurt; also, I feared that going through the rest of the war, however long it would be, I didn't know if I was prepared enough to run that supply section without him. He had trained me so well that I was able to do it. I had only been in for two years but with the unit, a year and a half. I didn't find out at first it was him. When I did, I was looking at the sky with the sun going down and smoke clouds everywhere. I couldn't believe it was him."

In Afghanistan, people were not getting injured or killed. Iraq was a different story. On that helicopter out of Iraq, I was laying horizontal. I could see the ground lift off, and all I could think was, *are we almost there? Are we almost there?*

The pain I felt seared right through me like hot coals. We landed and people rushed to us. Someone put a mask on me and that is all I remember until coming to, many hours later. I woke up in a tent surrounded by empty beds. I looked ahead and saw that the sheet was flat on one side.

Something missing—my leg.

Tears collected. Two of my Marines were standing there, looking down at me and trying to smile as I came to. One of them grabbed my hand as a kind gesture and I would not let go.

He said, "You need to let go…we need to go."

I pleaded weakly, "Don't leave me…"

Brian Lafferty and others were going to Baghdad and hearing conflicting stories about me. Someone who witnessed the explosion shook his head in despair when asked if he thought the leg could be saved.

Once in Bagdad, Brian called me on the satellite phone. We talked for a few minutes. I was completely out of my mind with pain and crying. Brian said something that made me laugh in a daze and then he whispered, "Goodbye." My hand still shook as I held the phone like it was the lifeline to my Marines during these terrifying minutes.

Over the next hours, the pieces of the disastrous puzzle came together. Once the first explosion tossed me into the air and shattered my body, Brian Alaniz rushed to get medical equipment. He felt a blast beneath him, a landmine, that obliterated the bones in his left leg, making it impossible to repair.

In his own words: "I would have to say that there were a few moments I would consider the scariest for me. The first was right after the explosion went off under me. I rolled over on my back and looked around and where there had been other corpsmen, there was no one. I didn't know if they had all been killed. I called for a corpsman but since after the explosion went off, they were given orders not to move, no one came. I remember picking my head up and looking at some of the vehicles we had driven in about ten feet away and seeing other corpsmen looking back at me, but they couldn't come help me. I started to think, *this is how I am going to die.* The other moment would have to be when they finally got me on a stretcher and loaded into the ambulance.

"I asked, 'How bad is it?', and someone said, 'You're going to be fine.' I cringed at the words. That is what the medical officer told us to tell anyone that was severely injured so that it wouldn't cause them to panic, and we could keep their breathing down and keep the blood flow at a constant level. I knew my injuries were pretty bad; I just didn't know how bad. The last one would have to be when we finally got medevacked back to Kuwait and after taking the X-rays, the doctor informed me that the bones in my leg were too shattered to repair and that they were going to have to amputate.

"I thought it was all a dream. I started to think, what will I do? How am I going to tell my wife and family? What are they going to think? The most encouragement I received was when I started to rehab and found out about prosthetic legs. I know it sounds like I am dumb, but I had never thought of or known about prosthetics! I had thought I was going to spend the rest of my life in a wheelchair.

"There is a saying we corpsmen follow: 'A corpsman will go through the gates of hell to get his Marine.' Corpsmen are trained to answer the call of our wounded Marines. I wouldn't have done anything different."

CHAPTER 8
FIGHTING FOR LIFE...SOMETIMES

WHEN I GOT to Germany, a whole team assessed me. This was eighteen years ago, and the military was unprepared for what was going to happen in Iraq. We learned from that series of events with me as a practice case. I would end up in Germany for ten never-ending days. My lungs collapsed. They were running through a flurry of questions first about my medical history. If I ever had surgery. If I had been put under. Any chronic conditions or allergies? They were removing a tube of the anesthesia and that is when my lungs collapsed. Here I am with no right leg. My left leg was broken. My right arm was broken. I couldn't go anywhere. I could barely move without wincing in excruciating pain I had never felt before. I would wake up after surgery with tubes down my throat. I was intubated. I went to touch the tube and the nurse screamed at me not to make a move. It felt like someone was choking me. I had this plastic tube pressing my tongue down. I felt the tube every time I swallowed. Between every breath, pain erupted. Then this fucking tube.

All I could do was cry and cry. I wanted the tube out of my throat. My parents weren't there yet. I had heard about Brian, but I didn't know where he and others were in the hospital. I was alone. I was in the ICU in front of the nurse's station. A clock read 2:00 p.m., 2:17, 3:00, 4:00, 4:20, 7:00, 9:00. …It just went on and on to 10:00, 11:00, 12:00 a.m. The light in the hallway was off. I saw the nurse's station light. Awake in all this indescribable pain.

The morphine was not helping.

I remember at around 2:00 in the morning, losing all hope. I had cried so hard. I was actually apologizing to myself for being ready to take my own life.

I silently talked to my parents, sisters, the other Marines before deciding to hold my breath. That was the only power I had to end it all! I remember hearing the nurses laughing once, and I'm sure I was not the subject of their shared humor, but I thought, *this is not the time to fucking laugh at anything!* I called for the chaplain at 2:00 in the morning. I couldn't talk, so I wrote it down with my left hand, which looked like chicken scratch because I was right-handed.

The nurse said, "You're not getting the chaplain right now."

I threw the pen on the floor, and she left in frustration. I don't think she was very empathetic. In reality though, the pain was so immense, she may have been sincere without me feeling it. That poor woman had not done anything wrong.

I started holding my breath.

I wanted to die.

Of course, after seconds, the stupid machines were going off, so the nurses rushed in. It's kind of humorous now how flimsy my "suicide attempt" was. I tear up thinking of those hours. After the nurses rushed in, I slept for an hour and a half or so. Then I pointed at the tube and one of the other nurses, who was simply exceptional, attended to me. I then pointed at the clock.

She said, "You want to know if the tube can come out?" I looked at her with desperation, nodding. "I'll have to talk to the doctor." And would you believe that very doctor lives in San Antonio now?

That afternoon, he came in and said, "We can take the tube out. What I want you to do when I take the tube out is start coughing."

I could feel that tube coming up through my chest, it was so long. I was horrified to see how much of that plastic had been in my body.

I had to stabilize before they could fly me back to the States, and I had no idea when that would be. One of the nurses, Jennifer, pushed in a cart overflowing with bandage and gauze. Jennifer was crying. The doctor told her to "step out of the room" if she was going to "keep losing it." Three others walked into the room.

I said, "What is going on? Why is she crying? I don't think I can deal with any more pain." I could feel my heart rate accelerating.

The doctor said, "Eric, we need to change your bandages. Your wounds are still open. Some of the bandage has stuck to your tendons and muscles. I am not going to lie to you. I will give you something for the pain, but it may not work well. This is going to hurt." After a beat, he said, "Where do you want to start first?"

Oh, I had a choice?

I said, "Just do whatever you have to do."

I braced myself against the bed railing. Jennifer sat down next to me. She put her hand over my hand and said, "Look at me, please."

They started changing bandages on my left leg and then got up to my stomach. I wailed. It was unbearable, and I bit down on my pillow. Jennifer couldn't even look at me after a while. The doctor arrived at my amputation, and I am surprised I didn't pass out. It was horrific. It was so sharp like being stabbed repeatedly with that gauze touching the nerves and muscles. It was hard for that whole team, I'm sure. I have a knot in my throat right now while describing this—it brings back a lot of memories that hurt my heart. Going into combat, some of us "expect" to get injured, but we can't exactly rehearse or simulate the full experience of losing limbs or losing people.

My parents found out about my accident on that Saturday through a maze of fragmented information apparently. As they were getting dressed for my cousin's wedding, they had two voice-mails from being out that morning; one from the San Antonio Police Department, leaving a callback number, and one from the United States Government. My dad humorously asked if my mother was "wanted" for something, and she thought he might have been "wanted" for an old crime during his drinking days!

Dad got ahold of someone from the San Antonio Police Department, and they urged him to stay by the phone for a call from the "sergeant." They fidgeted around the house with anxiety crackling in the carpet underneath them.

The tradition of the Alva men was to serve our country and I had followed. A cousin was wounded in Normandy Beach and had a metal plate in him.

My parents were watching CNN and they announced that two Naval personnel were wounded. Not Marines. The wounded were me and Brian. But Mom and Dad were convinced one of them was in trouble with the law. Dad went to the bedroom and Mom went into the kitchen to make a sandwich. The phone rang, and a sergeant from the Marine Corps spoke very formally to my mother, stating that he was from the base in California and needed to speak to the father of Marine Staff Sergeant Eric Alva. Now, this is only a day or two into the war and she was aware that it had started. She told him she was my mother.

He said, "I regret to inform you..." That is all she heard... or would allow herself to hear. My father heard her screaming. Dad ran into the kitchen to see her on the floor on her knees, screaming. She believed that I was dead. My father grabbed the phone from the counter and tried to pick up the conversation. The sergeant was holding and told him that I was injured. He gave Dad the details, which were slim. They could not say for sure where I was.

My dad kept repeating, "So, he's alive? He's alive?"

Dad called my sisters, Kathy and Laura, urging them to come to the house. Then other family members poured in. It was chaos, according to my dad, and mainly because they didn't want to ruin my cousin's wedding. They didn't want people to panic, but all they knew was that I was "alive." They didn't know the scope of my injuries or where I was being cared for. They made a series of calls and got the runaround—no concrete information. They stayed up all night, waiting for more info. This was the weekend, so no one was in the office anyway.

My mother would periodically say, "Eric is gone. My son is gone! …ERIC IS GONE!" My dad tried to be hopeful.

The next day, a Navy officer showed up at the door. My sisters opened the door and my mother just reached out and grabbed the man. "Is he dead? Is he dead?" she shouted. He backed up and asked her politely if he could come in. "Tell me right now!"

This man didn't know the answer. He explained what he knew—that I had stepped on a landmine, suffered blood loss, and was flown to a hospital in Germany.

Mom went berserk. She couldn't handle it. She called her doctor and informed him that she just couldn't function, so he put in a prescription for valium. I'm glad she had dosed up a bit because in less than twenty-four hours, the media descended on their doorstep. Our family became the focus of the war. Personnel tried to discourage my parents from going to Germany, as they insisted that by the time they got there, I might have been back in the air heading to the US. All the military knew was that I was conscious when I was airlifted. Sadly, two of my sisters had lost sons prematurely. My mom remembers one of the comments being, "You still have your other kids." Naturally, she wanted all her kids alive.

That day, the nurse came in to tell me that my parents were on the phone. I cried hysterically as soon as I heard my mom's voice. Remember that I had told her I would come home in one piece. I said, "I'm sorry, Mom, I'm sorry."

She said, "Why are you sorry?"

"I broke my promise to you!"

CHAPTER 9

FAMOUS FACES, DARK PLACES

Y TIME IN Germany was simply a blur of pain and torment. I had no idea what would happen when I was stable enough to be moved to another facility and what awaited me outside this cavern of mayhem, the consequences of war.

Once back in the States, many of us wounded Marines and Navy were taken on a bus to National Military Medical Center in Bethesda, Maryland. I was the last one to get collected from the bus and it was because of the media swarming around to get a glimpse of me. They needed to secure the perimeter and get me out safely. Four people lifted me up and put a brown military blanket over my face. In no time, through the thin blanket, my ears were assaulted with the sound of cameras flashing.

A new team of doctors had to assess me, and I refused. I was tired of people touching me. I didn't have my parents there yet. No one. There was a corporal in the next bed just staring at me like I was a behaviorally challenged alien.

The doctor stomped off and called my dad, who urged, "Eric, you need to do what they say. Put this in God's hands. Don't be difficult."

The war had been going on for two weeks. My parents were trying to get plane tickets and a place to stay. Southwest donated their flights, which helped them more quickly book a room.

When my parents saw me in that hospital, they just lost it. My dad took one look at me, turned around and ran out. My mom rushed to my bedside. I was asleep. It might have been too close to home for my dad. He had seen many friends die in Vietnam. When they went looking for him, he was on his knees in the chapel.

PTSD is all about triggers that take you back to a crisis.

Sighing, my dad recalls, "We got to Bethesda in the middle of the night when we were permitted to be escorted in. I saw the sheet flat, and his toes and fingers were black from being burned by the explosion. I turned around and ran out. Eric needed socks, so I went to the store. It was pouring rain and I sobbed uncontrollably, asking God for strength. I brought him two six-packs, not thinking he only had one foot now. I also brought him a strawberry malt, which made me smile a little because he always loved malts."

The whole fifth floor of Bethesda was filled with Purple Heart recipients. No family member had an appetite. The floor just seemed so dire.

I woke up from a major surgery to remove my knee because they had to go higher in the "guillotine amputation," as there was not enough skin to close it up safely. I swear, I heard one of the doctors tell my mom they "had to take my arm." They were leaning toward a double amputation? This was just a nonstop nightmare—one in which the hairy monster inflicted unbridled pain. My life had been reduced to pain, surgery, and being unconscious. I went ballistic.

"You're not taking my fucking arm! You're not taking my fucking arm!" I shouted through grinding teeth. They calmed me down, insisting that nothing of the sort would happen.

I did an EKG, and the doctor detected a small hole in my heart. My parents were covering their heads. I thought, *what is going on now?* It was raw layer after layer of bad news concerning my body.

I was dying for fresh air.

My mom wheeled me outside for the first time in so many days, and the media closed in on us upon one step outside the entrance. I would never anticipate how many encounters I would have with media later on and mainly positive, but in these moments, I thought of all of them as self-absorbed, heartless beasts.

One night, the little nightlight was on in my room. I caught a glimpse of my mom's tear-stained face. She looked uncharacteristically aged. While I whimpered, she said, "Eric, what do you need? What can I do?"

I looked at her eyes with so much pain and whispered, "You don't want to know what I am thinking."

She said, "Don't say it. Don't say it."

I said, "I wish I died over there."

Then I would fall back asleep. My body would shake uncontrollably. My mom would stay overnight as much as she could.

Private First-Class Jessica Lynch was on the same floor, and her room was heavily guarded by military police. She was in bad shape, in shock. Jessica had been serving as a unit supply specialist when her convoy was ambushed by Iraqi forces during the Battle of Nasiriyah. She was seriously injured. Her subsequent recovery by U.S. Special Operations Forces on April 1, 2003, was the first successful rescue of an American prisoner of war since World War II and the first ever of a woman. I saw her once when I was getting an X-ray. I will never imagine what she went through. Our parents met one another in passing.

My mom had been in *The Washington Post*, on Oprah, and CNN. My sisters were taking turns to be with her. My dad had to go back to work. I was terrified at the thought of my mom leaving. She was the only one I permitted to bathe me. I really didn't know how I was going to take care of myself, so the thought of suicide was always returning. I couldn't hurt my parents though. My mother had gone back to school, and she was on her last semester close to graduating. I was always angry. The chaplain had to remind her that the "drugs are talking, not Eric."

People came out of the woodwork to visit me. Michael Jordan, Arnold Schwarzenegger, Donald Rumsfeld all showed up to the hospital. Congress, senators, generals who had served in Vietnam. As a grand finale, President George W. Bush and First Lady

Barbara Bush made a sizeable entrance. Secret Service came in to remove everything but Brian and I in our beds and placed tape around floorboards and windows. They brought in dogs to sniff the room. They instructed my parents to stay in the same place and not ask any questions or approach President Bush for anything, or "give him any gifts." The First Lady came in first, stepped in to give me a hug, and started crying. Then President Bush came in and thanked me for my service.

As an afterthought, President Bush said, "Look at it this way. Your leg was blown off for freedom and your country." Then he walked out of the room, leaving me flabbergasted.

And another flabbergasting incident: Do you know what Oprah Winfrey said via satellite as me and Brian were sitting there with blankets covering our laps, appearing on her show? "Now that your legs were blown off, what went through your mind?"

It would also come to the surface that the night before I got wounded, my mother had a dream that I was riding in the desert with my legs propped up on the dashboard. She believes in dreams. Somehow this angle got to Oprah, who enthusiastically asked in Oprah fashion, "You had a premonition?" Oprah didn't get the answer she wanted. And my mom was certainly not used to this kind of attention. I must admit that this unforeseen attention annoyed me, too. For one, I didn't have a moment of inner peace to really process what was going on. When faces weren't staring down at me, the cards, balloons, and flowers did their part of filling the room like a fresh graveyard plot. Then some of the words I heard and read portrayed pure sensationalism and exploitation. Not most exchanges, which were sincere and laced with admiration, but enough that made me grimace.

I will say that I was very touched by a group of young Marines who drove from Quantico to DC because they wanted to meet me in person.

CHAPTER 10
REVIVING THE PURPLE HEART

I HAD GONE INTO the Marine Corps bootcamp as an E1 and left bootcamp as an E2 in rank. After six months, I was an E3 (lance corporal). Nine months later, I was put up on a meritorious board and promoted to corporal.

Back in Somalia, every morning, anyone who was E1, E2, or E3 had to put kerosene in about 200 huge barrels of shit and stir with an engineering stick until the shit burned, but I had been promoted to an E4 just in time, so I did not have to do this. I moved up quickly and amassed several ribbons. Before my third-year mark, I was put up for a Navy and Marine Corp Achievement medal. I received two more within the next year and a half. By the time I got to the staff academy with 125 staff sergeants, I was walking around with four metals.

I had barely walked into the room, and I was bombarded with comments like, "Who did you have to blow for those medals?" Bullying and the military go hand in hand at every ranking even though we're all supposed to be badasses. Right before crossing into Iraq, I had received my fifth medal for war preparation. All the while, I was not proving myself to other people. I didn't want people to know about these awards. At the same time, I was running and getting myself into the physical condition. My point is, I worked damned hard to be an E6!

Sometimes I feel guilty about what I have that other veterans don't. Was I given way too much? Well, three hours into war, I got severely injured.

My dad will tell you that I freaked out when they came to give me the Purple Heart. I cried, "I didn't fucking earn that!"

My dad was at my bedside gently urging me to take it. What

had I actually done? In my mind, I had gotten out of my vehicle and stepped on a landmine. At the time, I felt that only Brian Alaniz could relate. It helps a lot when you have someone going through the same things. A doctor or physiologist can only tell you what they know from books. Talking to someone who knows what pain you're going through, the same difficulties you're having, helps tremendously because you know you're not alone. Nevertheless, I repeatedly apologized to Brian because if it weren't for me, this wouldn't have happened to him.

His response is always the same: "It was not your fault. In war, bad things happen that you can't control. I was doing my job like I was trained to: Respond when my Marines call for a corpsman."

CHAPTER II
LOYAL LONE STAR

WHAT IS INJURY besides physical pain? A great deal of inconvenience at minimum. For example, when I had to piss, I could never get up to go to the bathroom. I don't know how many trips my poor mother made with a full bedpan.

Landing back in Texas, four women from the Air Force came on the plane to help me off. The media crowded together behind the fence. I recognized the faces of my Aunt Diane and other family members. My mother nudged me to give a thumb's up. They crammed me in an ambulance, and when I got to the hospital, they said they had to "quarantine" me. All these people came in full medical gear. Someone thought I was coming straight from Iraq, and they were worried about infectious disease.

A sign on the door said, "Quarantine: No Visitors."

Thankfully the "quarantine" didn't last past my complaint. My childhood friend, Hector, was one of the first to visit though we had not been in touch for quite some time. I had not seen Hector in years. He was now a police officer for the City of San Antonio. After arriving on a Friday into San Antonio, and going the weekend with no visitors, the following week, my quarantine lifted. I had so many visitors come from everywhere. Even people I did not know.

Mike and Brian were some of the first from my unit to visit me. I had already been in the hospital for several months by the time I saw Brian Lafferty and Mike, back from Iraq, come into my room. As soon as Mike saw that my leg was missing, his heart sunk into pure despair behind the poker face. He called the visit "almost soul-crushing." Prior to that, Mike knew that I was an avid marathon runner, always running, and extremely physically fit. We had always joked about my perfect scores in the fitness tests.

I was getting released from the hospital and going into an in-patient rehab facility. They followed me, determined to discuss how I was doing. My mom had gone around and checked the rehab facilities to pick one for me. The one she picked I really hated. By the time they met with me, I had already lost my mind.

I made everyone jump through hoops to get me into a different facility. Brian and Mike didn't get further than that lobby. There was just darkness. San Antonio got into the war casualty business as time went by. I was the first one and the only marathon runner in the room. These rehab places were filled with elderly people recovering from hip replacements.

Ultimately, I made it to HealthSouth Rehabilitation Institute of San Antonio (RIOSA), a modern, well-lit facility. They were trying to get me going with prosthetics. They asked me to put weight on it and it was torture! It would be oozing. Then they would want me to put the socket on and do rehab. Before leaving my room to return to California, Brian sobbed when he couldn't get his words out. It's safe to say we were both prepared for difficult military tasks in whatever environment you threw us in. But your body does not, cannot, rehearse pain from injuries.

I recall that for the first month in Kuwait, we didn't have showers. We had a water jug. The desert could be 98 degrees by 3:00 p.m. and then drop to 40 degrees by 3:00 a.m. Finally, I got so fed up, I asked one of the Marines to put the canister of water on top of the vehicle for me because I could not reach it.

He said, "What are you doing?"

I said, "Taking a shower."

He gasped, "But it's like forty degrees out here!"

I insisted, "I need a shower."

I would quickly strip down to flip-flops and stand on a wooden pallet. Slowly, I would open the nozzle to the water jug and wet myself. I would then close the nozzle and use a bar of soap to lather up. After that, I would open the nozzle to rinse off and then dry off as quickly as possible because it was so damned cold. You must realize that in the first few weeks in the desert, there were no showers for us to use, so I cannot recall how many days or weeks I went without a shower.

All told, between all my deployments, I spent five months in war. My father served one year straight in battle, in combat. I can't imagine enduring the conditions from the mosquitoes to the rain and humidity. He survived the 1968 Tet Offensive when during the lunar new year (or "Tet") holiday, North Vietnamese and communist Viet Cong forces launched a coordinated attack against a number of targets in South Vietnam. The U.S. and South Vietnamese militaries sustained heavy losses before finally repelling the communist assault. The Tet Offensive played an important role in weakening U.S. public support for the war in Vietnam.

I came home to an overwhelming heroes' welcome. My dad did not. Two very different times in history.

My mom was always a strong advocate for me to get better, but sometimes, she would minimize my pain or complaints. I had drainage coming from my leg, and she would say, "That's just the healing process." *Well, how the fuck do you know*, I would be thinking, *let me cut your leg off!*

The first year, your limb changes volume so you go through different fittings. It's frustrating because you want one that fits. I've been in my current version for five years. I don't have much of a limp.

When I tell people I've been injured, some reply, "I didn't even know you were missing your leg." It's the equipment, the therapy I've undergone. A combination has helped me get to where I am today.

When I first got out of the hospital, I was having drainage at the bottom of the stump (or "residual limb"). My mom did everything in her power as a mother to comfort me and make the pain go away. I was not always nice to her. She really meant well, and I truly believe that when I got hurt, so did she emotionally and mentally. But she was the best caregiver a son could ask for.

One person who was able to laugh with me about these caregiver episodes was Colonel Dr. James Ficke. What an amazing, angelic doctor! He served as the U.S. Army surgeon general as the senior advisor on policy and personnel for orthopedics and extremity injuries for seven years. Dr. Ficke has acted as a consultant to the Army surgeon general and served as chief medical officer of the Combat Support Hospital in Mosul, Iraq, treating more than 600 U.S. soldiers and Iraqi patients. Basically, I trusted him with my leg and life!

Months went by.

I was experiencing so much pain because I still had sutures in. I got back into the prosthetic and started walking. I got home and my leg had opened up again. It was leaking. Honestly, this is a process. I went back to the doctor at the end of 2003, and they found more sutures. I had to stay in the hospital overnight on New Year's Eve. I wanted to go into the new year walking, but I was not able to. Spring rolled around and in April of 2004, I had my final surgery to work on my amputation.

Dr. Ficke insisted that I take an epidural to be awake for this surgery. I could see the whole procedure through the lights. My leg was in a vertical position in vice grips. He found three more sutures. Altogether, nine sutures had been left in my body since my surgery from the battlefield.

It would be a long road back to skiing and scuba diving, and thanks to Dive Pirates and Disabled Sports USA, I got back to these activities in a more limited fashion, but I could not run anymore. I feel like that part of me died the day I was injured. It still makes me sad when I see people running around all the favorites in San Antonio.

My father, who had been absent during my childhood, did

show up for these tough times. In fact, he took me to therapy. "During the first few physical therapy sessions, Eric was in a wheelchair, and he hung his head down, just pumping morphine into himself," Dad said. "I would say, 'Eric, pick up your head and be proud!' He couldn't. It hurt me to see that flat pajama leg. I hated that sight. Losing that leg ripped out his heart. He said, 'Look at me, Dad. What am I going to do?' I encouraged him to motivate himself like he had motivated his Marines. I knew his life depended on it."

PART II
IN SOLIDARITY

CHAPTER 12
DECORATED HISTORY

ACCORDING TO COUNCIL on Foreign Relations, among enlisted recruits, 43 percent of men and 56 percent of women are Hispanic or a racial minority. Female recruits are consistently more diverse than the civilian population; they are also more diverse than male recruits. In 2016, the Defense Department lifted all restrictions on the roles women can perform in the military.

With the mission of the U.S. military being to preserve the country's peace and security and provide defense, am I going to do a better job as a white man? What about because I am Native American and Hispanic? Straight or gay? None of this matters on the job. I did not think about it until years after my retirement. I didn't think about all the people who were hiding their personal lives while protecting the freedoms of Americans in the civilian world.

In World War II, you had a lot of women going into the military for the first time. Margaret Cammermeyer was Norwegian and when she was still a baby, the Nazis invaded. Cammermeyer started active duty as an Army nurse in 1963. After training and serving abroad, she volunteered to go to Vietnam, where she ultimately became the head nurse of the neurosurgical intensive care unit. After Vietnam, when she was back stateside, married, and pregnant with her first child, she was forced into taking an involuntary discharge because military policy dictated that women with babies could not serve in active duty. While raising four sons and working at VA hospitals in Washington, Cammermeyer earned a master's degree in nursing at the UW in 1976. But she sought something more.

In 1988, Cammermeyer became chief nurse of the Washington State National Guard. Around that time, she met her future wife, Diane Divelbess, and her personal life became clear. During a security interview to vet her as a candidate for the War College, she revealed her sexual orientation.

And let's go back two whole centuries before that. In 1777, Benjamin Franklin went to Europe to get professional military people to come over and train General Washington's army. One of them was Gen. Friedrich Wilhelm von Steuben, who had to flee Prussia on charges of sodomy. It has been widely said that he was openly gay in the military and in the darkest days of the Revolutionary War. Both Franklin and Washington are thought to have known about his orientation and welcomed him with open arms because of his military qualifications. He became the father of the US Army, and the drill manual that von Steuben wrote for the Army is still partially used today. He has a statue right outside the White House.

There is much more to this historical homosexual relationship, but the point is though sodomy was a crime in colonial America, romantic relationships between men were widely tolerated until the 19th century. Then in the 20th century, the US military began to officially discriminate against people suspected to be gay.

In my household, we have lots of memorabilia tied to LGBTQ military—if no other history of our lives in service is recorded, believe me, my husband, Danny, is preserving it on the second floor of our house in the foyer and across two bedrooms!

You would see a picture of Patricia Rose, who was the highest-ranking officer to come out, a major general. We met her and she is married to her partner, who was also in the Navy. They had to make sacrifices to support each other's careers and kept everything totally hidden.

Army Reserve Officer Tammy Smith was promoted to the position of Brigadier General on August 10, 2012. In doing so, she became the first gay general to serve openly in the U.S. military.

Finally, we have a picture of three gay World War II veterans.

Frank, Jack, and John, who wrote *The Church and the Homosexual*. We placed a wreath at Arlington in their honor.

As I look around this room full of such memorabilia, I see an expansive understanding of my own history that I didn't have while serving my country under Don't Ask, Don't Tell. So deep was my desire to be an outstanding Marine, being authentic had been secondary.

In 2004, back in San Antonio, I was still in the Marine Corps. I didn't know if they would officially kick me out for being injured. I wasn't married. I didn't have a significant other. All I could think was, *who is going to take care of me?* I felt very vulnerable. Then that thought road went to, *who is going to love me now?* I was scared about my future when I left the hospital after seven months. Thoughts of suicide flooded my mind over and over. I couldn't do that to my parents and sisters though. As time went on, I knew I would get physically stronger. Depression was a small increment of everything that took place in all those months, but I did experience a few months of only sadness.

Then I finally said, "I will not live like this. I'm alive. I am LIVING!"

I started to get up at 5:30 in the morning to go swimming from 6:00 to 7:00, go back home and then sleep for a while. I knew I had to do something to get out of this mental loop. I had to return to California to turn in the key to my house, pick up my car and other stuff. My whole unit was home, so I knew this would be the first time they would see me in mobile shape. I was having problems with my leg, and I could not wear my prosthetic. I stopped by the supply warehouse, and I could not hold it together while saying goodbye. All these men were sobbing. I told them I was happy they all made it home.

My views on the war did change. In March 2004, the one-year anniversary of my injury, Amy Dorsett, a reporter for *San Antonio Express-News*, wanted to do an updated story of my progress.

We did the interview in March of 2004. I was getting ready to start school in the fall. President Bush was up for reelection. Amy asked me how I felt about the war, and I said that my views had changed, and I was against it now. I told her, "I will always support the men and women in uniform." She then asked me whom I was voting for. I said, "I don't know."

As time went on, I looked for the story in the newspaper, but it never came out.

In June of 2004, I was invited to speak at the Republican State Convention. I agreed and went in uniform, which landed me in a pot of hot water because this was against military policy. For the benediction, they took a picture of me backstage as I bowed my head and prayed. The next morning, I was scheduled to return to the convention and give the "Pledge of Allegiance" to the Daughters of the Republic of Texas. Well, the newspaper finally ran my March interview, but the piece did not feature a friendly update on my life. The front page screamed, "Warrior Against War" alongside my picture and continued to infer that I would be voting for Democrat John Kerry for President, which was inaccurate, or rather, dead wrong. Plus, an enormous picture, as if the headline and my name weren't enough to call attention!

People blamed *Express-News* and Amy Dorsett for sensationalizing that I had issues with the war. At the convention that afternoon, organizers openly called attendees to boycott the paper. No one knew I was gay. I didn't come out until 2006. I was living, driving, and moving on with life in a new house—they did not feature any of this positive information. Other reporters were calling my sisters at their workplaces.

Amy called me and I confronted her about manipulating me into doing an interview and then running something so far off the mark. I was infuriated. She tried to apologize. We didn't speak again. I later heard that she passed away from MS. My family gave her numerous interviews—we had allowed her total access and we trusted her.

On that Sunday morning, I received a phone call from the sergeant major of my unit, instructing me to come into the base first thing Monday morning. When I arrived, I was taken in the commanding officer's office and told to "stand at attention." Next thing I knew, I was being read my Article 32 rights—I had broken the uniform code of military justice. I "went to a political event and spoke in full dress uniform still on active duty." This was equivalent to treason or being a conscious objector. In the end, I received a warning, but this stained me—getting read my rights by the entity I almost gave my life for. I was gearing up for medical retirement on June 30, just seventeen days later. It was a bizarre series of events.

With all this behind me, I built the house of my dreams. I started over literally from the foundation up. I signed the paper-work on June 26, 2004, for the house and then retired on June 30, four days later. I decided to go back to school in the fall. I took seven classes the first semester. I threw myself into education.

And I started dating someone.

I had been navigating the chat rooms a little bit and got on gay.com. I met Darrell Parsons, a social worker in Wyoming. On the chat, he asked me if I was "really gay." I was kind of mystified. This was on a gay chat! Well, at thirty-eight, I was the first person that he was declaring his gayness to. His parents were deceased. He had not told friends. I found this hard to believe.

Then I said, "Well, I have something to tell you."

He replied, "What?"

I said, "I am missing a leg. I lost it in Iraq." At first, he thought I was kidding.

We traded pictures and talked every day on the phone for months before meeting. Then I finally encouraged him to come and visit me. I picked him up from the airport and he made a comment about my height, but we hit it off. We decided to do a long-distance relationship.

CHAPTER 13
A NEW EDUCATION

DECIDED TO INTRODUCE Darrell to my family on Thanksgiving, and there was only one glitch. My father didn't know I was gay. I asked my mom to tell my father. They went for a drive, and she said, "Have you ever noticed that our son is always by himself?"

Dad replied, "Yes, but he is shy."

She pressed, "You ever notice that he never goes on dates?"

"He's not met the right girl!"

She just laughed and said, "Your son is gay."

He paused and said, "It's okay. He's my son." Then looking out the window, he chuckled. "I used to get on bulls when I was a kid. I put Eric on one and he froze. Before he got wounded, he would come in on leave, and I was retired from Lockheed Martin, fully present. My light bulb never turned on that he was gay."

Mom called to give me this uneventful report. Everyone got along during the holidays. That following spring, I invited Darrell to move in with me. I bought a one-way plane ticket to go and help him load up. We drove his truck back and he became a Texan! It's so amusing though because Darrell was the one who introduced me to the Human Rights Campaign (HRC), and I never knew what the blue and yellow equal sign meant before him. I was his first boyfriend and he had not been out before me, but he paid serious attention to politics and world events. Now, Darrell is very well-known in San Antonio. He's a huge advocate, sits on many boards and helps to improve the lives of LGBTQ youth.

In the meantime, my doctor enlisted me to talk to other amputees. I got certified by the Amputee Coalition of America to become a peer counselor. Today, almost 2 million Americans have experienced amputations or were born with limb difference. Another 28 million people in our country are at risk for amputation. Amputation of the leg—either above or below the knee—is the most common amputation surgery. I could empathize with all these men and women who had been in war and lost limbs. I tried to reassure them about their lives ahead. I didn't reveal anything about my personal life at the time even though I was always bombarded with questions about dating and having children.

I moved into the new house alone, and I was living next to a retired Air Force pilot, who was now a Baptist minister, and his wife. After Darrell moved in, I guess they noticed that he was not only "visiting." They started asking me who Darrell was. I told them he was my "roommate from college" and that he would be living with me for a while. I hadn't yet reconciled being gay with being in the military under staunch homophobic policies, with my new-found freedom, same-sex relationship and civilian life. I was busy trying to put the pieces together as a disabled man first. This was only reinforced by my community, as nearly every time I would go to a restaurant or a ticketed event, someone recognized me as the "hometown hero" and would take care of my bill. I never wanted this kind of attention. I'll never forget all the kindness though.

When Darrell wanted to put that colorful equal sign on my car, I barked that I didn't want any damned stickers on my car. But when I changed my major to social work and immersed myself in the program, I started to see how diverse I was: gay, disabled, veteran, Latino and Native American.

In the spring of 2006, Darrell came home from work, and I showed him that I slapped the HRC sticker on my car, to his surprise. I started to pay attention to what was happening in the country. We went through the process of painfully watching the state of Texas banning same-sex marriage. My Baptist neighbors put up a sign containing little stick figures of "man + woman = marriage." At the same time, I was heavy into social justice coursework centered on people being who they are. This started to seal my next phase in life. We were watching TV and I was getting incensed.

Darrell said out of the blue, "If you ever want to do something with your life that makes a difference, do it now while people know who you are. You are the first American who was injured in the Iraq War. You fought for this country. You are gay."

The smartass in me piped back, "You just want to keep getting free meals!" It wasn't a nice thing to say or even remotely close to Darrell's intentions and I knew it as soon as I said it.

Within days, things were getting intense. They were passing constitutional bans on same sex marriage under the George W. Bush campaign. They were pushing referendums in all the states to drive out voters. It was a wedge issue. It hit me that I had gone to war for my country. My commander-in-chief at the time was George W. Bush and now, here is the country and a candidate using these types of issues to discriminate against us and they're winning elections, which made me angry.

We were sitting in Darrell's office talking further about it and he said, "The commander-in-chief, who is passing these constitutional amendments, was at your bedside giving you your Purple Heart!"

I said, "Who would I tell my story to? The local news?"

Darrell shouted, "No! Much bigger than that. Call the Human Rights Campaign and they will do something with you."

We were not out at the time as a couple. Even though I was out as an individual, we didn't feel like it was a safe time for us to be out. But that night, I tossed and turned with the weight of Darrell's words and everything going on in our nation. I started doing research on the Human Rights Campaign. I contacted Brad Luna, the communications director, introducing myself and that I wanted to help the organization in any way I could. Amazingly, I wasn't even thinking of Don't Ask, Don't Tell!

CHAPTER 14
POST-TRAUMATIC DISCOVERIES AND A FAMILY REUNION

SINCE EARLY CHILDHOOD, I had not seen both of my parents in the same room as often as I did after being injured. Both of them tended to me in the hospitals and rehab centers as much as they could. Both of them took me to therapy. And both of them took insults when I was out of my mind with pain and chaos. I lost my leg. They gained their love for one another again during this time.

It's clear that Dad had inadvertently pushed his family away as soon as he started making it due to what he experienced in the Vietnam War.

He adds, "I am a disabled veteran, 70% PTSD. There are scars of war that still live with me. My son will never forget what happened to him and I'll never forget what I saw."

But I know his PTSD started long before he put that uniform on. I remember stories such as his dad teaching him arithmetic and then backhanding him in the face when he wrote down the wrong answer. He volunteered for the draft to get away from him and went to war immediately. Dad was born in 1948. Vietnam was never a secure area. It was not bigger than the state of Illinois.

Once back in Texas, Dad went in uniform to his friend's house to see him after the war. His mother answered the door, thinking her son was with Dad. He had died in Vietnam and neither Dad nor the boy's mother knew at the time.

With all this trauma, loss, and corrosion of the family, I never dreamed that the whole family would be together again.

It takes an act of Congress to fire a veteran. Dad was physically, mentally, and spiritually bankrupt. He had prayed to God to take his life in his sleep. He was too ashamed to go on living yet too chicken to commit suicide. He merely wanted the pain to stop. He went to a convenience store with a plastic bag full of coins to buy a bottle.

"I used to say that the war killed me, but it was just a chapter of my life," he said. "My battle with alcoholism was much tougher. My past is my greatest asset. I never want to forget that feeling of uselessness that drove me to drink. I had empty quart bottles lying around my bed. I had no pride left. As I looked around, I was vomiting blood. Vomiting insanity. The obsession, the compulsion to drink, is removed by a God of your understanding."

Dad's spiritual work after seeing the blood and bottles that day paid off. He called my mother at work after not hearing her voice in ten years. She agreed to meet him for lunch. In truth, us kids told her *not* to go back to that living hell, even though he had been sober for years. We hadn't seen his sobriety enough. We didn't comprehend what he was like without drinking. He had destroyed our childhoods, so reconciliation wasn't a crystal-clear path.

He shares, "I visited my parents' gravesite four years after getting sober and said, 'I became the son you always wanted.' I sit now at the family table and think, I would have missed all of this love and connection if I had not gone through my program. On the phone I told Eric to 'leave the attitude and bring the gratitude.' My kids weren't giving me a chance. Time after time, alcoholics lie. It takes years to recover from abuse or what they saw, and my apologizing and becoming sober does not clean the slate, I realize."

My parents remarried, and my father redeemed himself. I brag about him all the time now in my speeches. His very sobriety took courage. Remarrying my mother as a better man was quite a stunning act, and as they say, it was pretty Texas-sized!

My father and I were two injured veterans. But modern times afforded me many more resources to heal than he had received. I never once thought I didn't get the right resources. With any organization it's a process. I was fortunate that I got injured early, which means the system was not overwhelmed. But then when dozens and hundreds were injured, the system became a conveyor belt. Getting approval for benefits went from fourteen days to forty-five days. All it takes is one person to go on the news with negative messaging and the whole system gets casted in a bad light. A veteran died in the waiting room. One story can change the world's perception. I have physical therapy on Tuesdays for my shoulder. To this day, I am in good hands with the federal government. Is it like that for all people? No. I see a psychologist once every six months, but I could go as often as I'd like. This last appointment, I just wanted to run down the clock and not talk. I didn't feel like saying what I knew I was already going through—I was injured in war, so I have nightmares and agitation. I've always been strong. People come to me all the time about the veteran in their family who is greatly suffering after surviving an explosion or a bullet wound and they're not seeking any kind of mental assistance. There is so much going on with that person.

CHAPTER 15

THE STRUGGLE TO ASK, TELL, SERVE

I WAS THE BEST man in my friend, Roger's wedding, which gave me hope that I would marry a man someday, too. I wasn't sure if that man would be Darrell. I remember when Roger informed me that he had gotten kicked out of the Marine Corps for being gay. He always felt he let people down, including his father, but he didn't. What a horrible notion to live with.

A few days went by and then Brad Luna from HRC replied, inviting me and Darrell to the HRC gala in San Antonio, Texas; and they would pick up the tab. We met Joe Solmonese, the president, for coffee at the hotel. He laid out the plan for how he saw me getting involved. We didn't have a sense of timeline, which was fine, because I was engrossed in my academic program and physical activities. I knew something would become of it, however. Filled with a sense of purpose, I was electrified.

A few months later, I flew to the DC headquarters and met with all the staff. When I walked in, dozens of people bowed their head to me. They also gave me a cupcake with a candle in it and sung "Happy Birthday." Strangers brought together by common goals toward making the world a better place. I got to know all of these people over the course of four days, ending with, "Merry Christmas, happy New Year! We'll contact you next year."

Joe Solmonese describes the movement at the moment: "During the Bush presidency and the years when the House and Senate were Republican-controlled, we were spending most of our time fighting the federal marriage amendment. When the Democrats took control of the House in 2006 was when we began to sort of feel we had the opportunity to move a proactive agenda.

At the top of that list was the passage of the Hate Crimes

Bill and the repeal of Don't Ask Don't Tell. That was around the time when the fight to repeal Don't Ask Don't Tell became more formalized and there was a chance to have a roadmap and chance to pass it into law."

Alas, Joe wanted me to directly advocate for the repeal of DADT. He saw my story as the perfect kickoff for that campaign to begin. In reality, the more excited I became, the less I thought about my personal relationship. Our lives were going to change dramatically. This would force Darrell out of the closet. Low and behold, when I said Darrell's name on TV, he was afraid of his family hearing it. He also expected someone to spray-paint ugly words on our garage door. Though I did receive hate mail from those who didn't believe in equal rights, the response was overwhelmingly positive.

But remember that I had a tight-knit group of Marines who I had not come out to. If they heard this information from a public forum, given everything we had been through together, I'm sure it would feel like I didn't trust them enough to tell them about the most personal parts of myself.

Before I talked to Brian Lafferty about it, he was worried I was going to take my life. The following year, after his son, Nick, was born, he asked me to be his godfather. I said, "If you and Lisa trust me that much and think of me that highly, I need to share something with you." I informed him that I was gay. He said he was "cool with it," but he needed to discuss it with Lisa. The next morning, as he promised, he called and said "Congrats." I got the esteemed job of gay godfather!

He adds: "We're Catholic and the Catholics and the LGBTQ aren't always on the same sheet of music. I got to see Eric in a different light. The movement against Don't Ask, Don't Tell gave Eric something to live for. It took him from losing so much—running, which was a really big thing for him, forced out of the

Marine Corps, which he was really great at, and then in the

blink of an eye, out and politically active with something to live for. I think about where he has come from. I'm filled with joy his life is so much more than that one, unlucky day in Iraq."

Darrell and I weren't the same after the activities took me away from home the majority of the time. But he has gone on to do so many courageous things. He found his niche in San Antonio with a youth group called Fiesta Youth, an LGBTQ support group. He was one of the founding board members. In 2013, a mom was looking for support for her teenage child who had just come out and there was no support group in San Antonio. She reached out to Darrell because of his resources at the LGBTQ Chamber of Commerce and in HRC. They started this group together, which has helped hundreds of kids since.

We grew exponentially as individuals and ultimately discovered we would be better off as friends.

CHAPTER 16
KEEPING UP APPEARANCES

MY ACTIVISM COULD have been anytime during the year, but I was very occupied with life. When Joe Solmonese called to ask me to come back to DC, Congress was gearing up to introduce the Military Readiness Enhancement Act of 2007, essentially to enhance the readiness of the Armed Forces by replacing the current policy concerning homosexuality in the Armed Forces, referred to as "Don't Ask, Don't Tell," with a policy of nondiscrimination on the basis of sexual orientation.

I got in that night calmly to my hotel, only to be greeted by a reporter from *The Washington Post*. I was starving, but I had to do this hour-long interview that would be released on the same day as my "out party" on "Good Morning America." That story in *The Washington Post* came out that Wednesday before "Good Morning America" was scheduled, so people in San Antonio would not have seen it.

Tuesday, I did an interview with ABC's Jake Tapper. Literally the news spread like wildfire while I was still in Washington DC. A reporter called me from San Antonio and left me a message, wanting to know if they could give local coverage to "anything."

They had covered me trying to walk and about my heritage, our military family. I simply told her that the "real news" to pull from would be on "Good Morning America."

When the story came out, I can't tell you what that day was like, from morning to midnight. Dozens of media outlets contacted me. My dad worked in civil service with other veterans from Vietnam and my mother was a teacher. People knew our name from generations back until present. When I had been injured, my parents received a great deal of attention, too. By coming out, I knew the limelight would be on all of us. Before I went to Washington DC, I prepared my parents for this. I wasn't going to cave into any pressure to not come out publicly, but I owed them notice.

My mom received comments like, "I saw your son on the news yesterday and I will pray for you!" Then others would say to my father, the Vietnam vet, "You must be very proud of your son!"

As expected, they were hearing it from all sides. One unifying theme between most of the news clips at least was that I came from San Antonio, Military City. Locals liked that.

For those who responded negatively, including some who had paid warm homage to me before, where was the same pat on the back or "thanks for your service?" I was the same man. In those same restaurants and stores that had treated me like a celebrity, some of the patrons would turn their head or look at their watch when I walked past. In the end, people started to see who I really was. That felt right. After that spot on "Good Morning America," people came up to me all the time—to the point that I couldn't get my grocery shopping done! I received mail from Australia, Israel, Canada, all over the world. We were still in the midst of two wars.

I think the capstone question in all my many interviews was: Why didn't you come out sooner?

Perhaps my response in *The Washington Post* not only sums up the dilemma but also, shows all the cards—the audacity, the hypocrisy, the sheer selfishness at play. "Eventually my notoriety—'the injured Marine'—will wear off. And I can almost hear it now, 'Oh, yeah, he's that gay Marine.' I'm okay with that. The truth is, something's wrong with this ban. I have to say something. I mean, you're asking men and women to lie about their orientation, to keep their personal lives private, so they can defend the rights and freedoms of others in this country, and be told, 'Well, oh, yeah, if you ever decide to really meet someone of the same sex and you want the same rights, sorry, buddy, you don't have the right.' That's one factor. The other factor is, we're losing probably thousands of men and women that are skilled at certain types of jobs, from air traffic controllers to linguists, because of this broken policy."

My grandfather, father, and I paid life-altering sacrifices in exchange for freedoms—freedoms that were ultimately denied to me in my thirteen-year military career.

When the war was going on, I was moved to the TDRL (Temporary Disability Retirement List). Technically, I was temporarily retired so when I decided to come out, another Marine approached me and said, "Do you realize what you've just done?"

I said, "No."

He continued, "Are you retired? They could move you back to active duty and start discharge procedures under Don't Ask, Don't Tell." I had TOLD on national television! I broke the law. In spite of that, no further action was taken because the powers that be were afraid of the negative publicity that would surely ensue.

I remember in 2004, my mother asking me if I watched the convention because she was so stoked by one of the speakers: a senator from Illinois, Barack Obama. She said, "He was unbelievable. I bet in four years, this man will be President!"

In 2007, campaign promises started to roll in regarding gay rights from Bill Richardson, Hillary Clinton, and Barack Obama. In 2008, Obama became President. We relied on him to turn the tide. I knew if we repealed Don't Ask, Don't Tell, we were opening Pandora's box. What would happen to same-sex couples that were married legally from Massachusetts and Vermont that were in the military? Respecting their benefits and rights? Their marriage was legal. We had to bring down the law for banning same-sex marriage.

In 2008, we saw the election of the first African American U.S. President, which moved the needle rapidly toward what was to come.

Joe Solmonese and I did a lot of lobby day visits and

conferences with members. We shared the good and the bad, needless to say! He wrote a book a few years ago confronting things that make you angry and how you strategically put your anger aside to get to the greater good. He claims that I was a lot of inspiration for that book, along with Judy Shepherd, who had lost her beautiful son, Matthew, to heinous, hateful violence. Joe has publicly thanked us numerous times for exhibiting the same qualities. Her in the fight to pass the Hate Crimes Bill and me, in my fight to repeal Don't Ask, Don't Tell. This is because he had to listen to Congress—yes, elected officials—saying things to us that just were so insulting and demeaning and so off-putting. Despite all the insults, we never lost sight of why we were there. We were given the privilege of being in the room with this member of Congress and if that person said they "didn't know anyone affected by a hate crime" or there "weren't any gay people in their district, or in the Marines," we didn't give in to the anger that would have understandably elicited. We never lost sight of what we were there to do. No matter how absurd or demeaning or insulting the question was, I had an answer designed to get the person we were talking to, to "yes." I told you I've had a loud mouth since I was a toddler! Only this time, I was using it for the greatest impact I could possibly make in this life.

Of course, Joe also witnessed my vulnerabilities during that time. Over the years, he has given me infinite advice. In his own words: "The thing about Eric and why he was such a powerful advocate is he is largely without an ego. He stepped into this for all the right reasons. He thought his story had the power to contribute to changing the law. You can go back to Lyndon Johnston signing the Civil Rights Bill and you have a bunch of people standing there mad at each other because someone got more credit. This is not unique to us, but when you're in it, it can be a little startling. One of the things Eric encountered that could be discouraging was people got into it with more of an ego, more of a desire to be somebody or make a name for themselves or get some credit. Eric wouldn't get it. Why is this person hogging the spotlight? Demanding to speak when not only do I think I should speak? Dan Choi is an example. He gets a lot of credit. He's considered the agitator compared to some of us methodically going step by step. He chain-linked himself to the White House. People called saying, 'Why didn't he chain link himself to McCain's front door because today, he is the obstacle, not Barack Obama?' In any fight like this, there is a group of people with an element of involvement that is self-promotion and ego—and I would never say they were less committed to the fight though. It was so foreign to Eric that he would be frustrated or disappointed."

Another thing you should know about Joe is that he trained with the U.S. Marine Corps…sort of. Every year, there is something called the "joint commission of civilian involvement" with Department of Defense. Approximately twenty civilians on a week-long trip where you join members of the defense community and go on a C130 carrier every day to a different military base in the country. You land on the base and do whatever the pros are doing on the base that day. Joe started at Quantico and did a day of what we would do in the Marines in basic training. It was so interesting for Joe to be in this setting with young people in the service. The army barracks in Kentucky with a bunch of eighteen-years-olds who had just enlisted, left home and learned about what life was like. Joe fully came to understand the sacrifice, but he also didn't want to enlist in the military! I, for one, am glad that he went on to do great things elsewhere like serve the Human Rights Campaign.

As we started to gain momentum with appearances on CNN, C-SPAN, and many other outlets, it didn't escape Marines like my friend, Lavon Peters. He recalls being in Iraq on his third deployment, where he saw my crazy face come on TV in the mess hall. I was advocating for the repeal of Don't Ask, Don't Tell. He was astounded that I was not only testifying but also, that I was at the forefront of this monumental change in the way that the military would operate and how individuals would serve.

Even though friends were watching, I wasn't always polished! My first speech lasted twelve minutes and it was supposed to be an hour, for instance. At the same time, most people didn't know that I was working at CVS to pay off some debt. That is how responsible I always was. I didn't wait on big-bucks speeches, as they didn't exist at the time. I got a call from UTSA in the social work program. A professor had known of me and thought to offer me this job for a ninety-day assignment. By law, this type of job has to be advertised, so she urged me to apply online, but I interviewed with her on a Thursday and got the job on Monday. I didn't have the experience working in the field, but she loved me. I was to do public speaking, too. The whole package sounded remarkable.

Six months in, I got let go because of the loss of funding for the position, but two months later, they found the funding to hire me back. Then I was approached with an opportunity to teach policy. I had no way of knowing that in 2020, a U.S. election year, transformative leadership would be the name of the stamp on this new decade.

CHAPTER 17

RETRIBUTION AND REPEAL

THE HAIR-RAISING MOMENT, or I should say the downward spiral, of getting DADT repealed was when the Senate voted in September of 2010 and the votes were not there to pass DADT. It was also the midterm elections and the invention of the stupid "tea party" was created. The House lost control, rewinding (in my mind) back to Republicans. I really thought we were done. Now, there was no way we would ever repeal DADT. Through my daily hard work, I kept asking why this discriminatory policy had been installed in our military branch in the first place. I'm privileged to let someone else answer this for a change!

Brian Lafferty responds, "I was in the Marines for twenty-two years and civil servant now for ten years. If you think about the Don't Ask, Don't Tell fight and things we all know to be false—gay soldiers are not man enough for the battlefield and all that shit—when it comes to Eric, they picked the wrong guy. There was nobody better at the Marine Corps thing than Eric. His Marines loved him. He was fantastic at his job. Supply is not shooting the enemy but this map of bureaucracy. Everyone is cheating the system and there are stupid deadlines. He was great at juggling that stuff. If you look at Eric's stack of ribbons, he's got more awards for being a great Marine than a lot of people who did it for a lot longer. He has a giant stack of awards for being great at his job. And around physical fitness, in the twelve years Eric was there, I think he only ran one PFT (physical fitness test) that wasn't perfect. It was like two points below. On a scale of 300, 300 being perfect, which is twenty pull-ups, the maximum number of sit-ups or crunches and a three-mile run in eighteen minutes or less, my best one might have been 250 and Eric's worst one might have been 296. Everything that was false about gay Marines serving openly, he proved wrong in one person. One person proved every one of those things wrong."

I will validate all this information; however, there is no way I could say it better than Brian.

Joe Solmonese and I were together on the morning President Obama signed the Don't Ask, Don't Tell Repeal Act into law. It was an incredibly emotional journey for both of us and we'd been through it together. There were long stretches of really inspiring, moving parts of the journey. There were a handful of men and women serving in silence or had been discharged and stepped into the fight. With them on the road in town hall meetings or meeting with members of Congress, it was inspirational. It was matched by really frustrating periods where I thought we were going to fail.

In the final six months, it was horrific. In 2010, we brought it to the Senate floor two or three times and failed. It wasn't until the lame duck session in December that we got the bill through the Senate on December 16. Obama signed it on December 22. Talk about cutting it close! There had been mounting pressure from the community to get it done and mounting pressure on us, and Joe in particular. If we failed, someone was going to be accountable. As HRC was the biggest entity spearheading the effort, it would surely be held accountable.

The behavior of others was unseemly when things got difficult, but I tried to never fall victim to that kind of behavior. It wasn't in my DNA to not only not give up, but also, not finger-point or second-guess or equivocate like some others. At the same time, I didn't need credit. There was a downside to the battles though, like when my family had to read negative comments from total strangers online about me. One man said, "So what, you lost your leg. Too bad you didn't die!" This is one that I couldn't help but respond to. I had one man stalking me for a while. He was calling me nonstop from a burner phone. The action would ramp up every time I made a TV appearance. I had to file a police report. I had to be aware of my surroundings. A few years ago, in a parking lot, I saw a reflection of someone coming behind me. I turned around swiftly. It was an older gentleman. He backed up. "I'm sorry. I'm sorry." I said, "What are you doing creeping up on me?" He admitted to recognizing me and following me out of the store.

CHAPTER 18
LOVE CONQUERS HATE

(SO PUT A RING ON IT!)

TH THE PRO -MARRIAGE movement building momentum, I couldn't help but think about love. I met Danny Ingram by pure accident in 2010. We were both working on legislation to repeal DADT. We were honoring Veteran Lobby Day, representing LGBTQ people and allies. When I noticed Danny then, I thought, *wow, what an attractive man!* Despite all this gay-centered action, I had thought Danny was a straight ally.

When we finally got to the repeal of DADT, I was on stage with President Obama. Danny was in the audience and already knew my story. We both knew exactly what the elimination of this discriminatory policy meant: Tens of thousands of LGBTQ service members would now openly serve. As of 2017, that number was 48,500, according to UCLA's Williams Institute.

The following year, I was single and got invited to New York City's HRC gala featuring Barbara Walters. I brought a date, who turned out to be a pain in the ass. I saw Danny. I walked on the silly "red carpet" and reporters kept asking for pictures of just me and urged my date to leave the carpet. I didn't hear the end of that incident. Then Walters was scheduled to introduce me, and I had no idea!

In 2013, Danny and I ran into each other again in Denver, Colorado. I was invited to be the keynote speaker for American Veterans Equal Rights, which he turned out to be the president of at the time. He had a leather jacket on tight around his upper body. At the hotel, I asked him if he wanted to get a drink and we chatted for two hours. The next night, when I was scheduled to go on the stage, I was getting ready for my speech. He said, "Can I ask you a personal question?" I said, of course. He pulled me outside the lobby and asked, "Before you leave, with your permission, can I give you a kiss?"

I was both flattered and tickled by this Southern gentleman from Atlanta. I said, "Sure," with a big smile.

The evening went on and it was a successful evening. I reached over with my right hand because he extended his left land. He thought I was making a gesture that would get me to his room that night. The next day was Sunday, and I was getting ready to leave. He carried some stuff to my car to help me. I reminded him about the kiss. He simply kissed me on the cheek...after all that anticipation!

We exchanged numbers. We talked day after day after day. The first thing I learned about Danny was that he went to school for theology and had set out to be a priest. I thought that was kind of hot! His favorite things in life are nature, trees, and actively helping to maintaining a healthy environment for wildlife, plant life, and people. I also learned that one of the reasons Danny had joined the military was they told him that he couldn't serve. Fortunately, he was sitting in a big room filling out paperwork, and no one was paying attention to him. The recruiter screamed, "Next question: Are you a homosexual? Everyone say, 'No!'" He went into the military because he wanted to do something for the world. He didn't want someone else to ever fight his fights—even the massive one for democracy, which he recognized that he valued during college after "meeting Jewish people for the first time." With the body to show for it, Danny was very into fitness in the military just like me. He earned a patch for excelling at fitness and he also had a sticker on his car: "Soldier for Life." Now, why shouldn't this upstanding gentleman who loves his country not been able to serve? He was willing, able, and eager to do something significant with his life and protect our nation's freedoms.

I really loved everything about this man.

I had to go to Honduras for a diving trip and I offered to visit him beforehand because honestly, I couldn't conceive not talking to him for a few days.

I drove to see Danny in Atlanta. I also drove to Denver once for an event.

When I drive, I don't wear the prosthetic because it starts to pinch and hurt. I call the leg "Facetious." On the way to see Danny, I put the leg in the front seat and put the seatbelt over it. I stopped in New Orleans. I chuckle thinking about the number of drunken Southerners who may have seen Facetious belted in next to me! In Alabama, I got pulled over by a trooper for going ninety or so miles an hour. I usually get let go because the police officer used to be a Marine, they see the military insignia on the license plate, or they recognize me from TV. On one occasion that I got pulled over, the police officer walked up and had a tiny Marine pin on. Sure enough, we got into the Marine talk, and he let him off with a warning. In Alabama though, I got a ticket!

Danny and I dated for a couple of years until he retired in 2016. The plan was to live together for six months as more of a trial because he is very traditional. (Thus, kissing my hand.) Well, we got married so that tells you how the trial went!

As to the reception of our marriage, note that Danny grew up in the rural South in a very conservative family. There were two religions: Baptist and Methodist, and they did not like each other. Religion was very important. All his family "knew" about homosexuality could be summed up as jokes, whispers, nudges about it being "the worst thing you can be." When he informed his parents that he was gay, his father was just crushed, devastated. Fortunately, Danny's stepmother said, "I just hope you don't ever have problems with anyone because I will kick their ass." She was the most supportive of our marriage. She is the only one who welcomed me into the family or even congratulated us.

It took a few years for Danny to confess that he had been wondering how to treat Facetious and me. He had dreams about a sharp bone sticking out of my leg. How gruesome! Despite his nightmares about what my leg would look like, it turned out to be a nothing for him. But he has always been cognizant of my leg.

When we moved into our new home together in San Antonio, the shower didn't have any handles or extra support. He was very concerned for my safety, so he installed suction handles on his own.

My husband and my dogs give me all the loving support I need. The reality is that if I had not used my voice in vehicles like the Human Rights Campaign, I would not have met Danny. Me standing at a podium made a direct line connecting us. I love Danny so much for being equipped to deal with my trauma and drama. I can't be easy. Ask my mother!

People have asked me what my main stressors are since I have a beautiful house and an even more beautiful husband. Nothing worth having in life is free. There is a cost for freedom. There is a cost for authenticity. There is a cost for love—particularly for the LGBTQ population. And sometimes the support and resources that bridge all the needs are scarce.

Danny has been advocating for such resources from the Veterans Affairs. His argument has been that you can't just put an LGBTQ person in a support group with other people because they're not going to feel comfortable in sharing it. The PTSD is the cost. Before 2010, service members had to maintain a lie afraid they would lose their job, their career, in a minute if someone found out. That's PTSD. You also have the PTSD from growing up in a country that tells you you're crap every day of your life. In working for a veteran service organization for LGBTQ, he is getting the VA to understand that there are specific unique needs for LGBTQ veterans that they need to develop programs for. If someone is in combat and is killed, will their partner back home be told? These real-life scenarios existed every hour of the day in the military.

When I think of my dad in Vietnam, dealing with PTSD in and of itself is enough. Fighting for the repeal of Don't Ask, Don't Tell held many implications. It wasn't just me having an axe to grind after stepping on a landmine. I had expanded my mind to fully understand numerous connecting points underscoring the quality of life for many and what they had to possibly compromise.

Another example is that the AIDS epidemic caused PTSD for an untold amount of LGBTQ people. The VA started sponsoring were discharged for being gay received a dishonorable discharge. This is not only an undesirable label—people lost their benefits.

You can now be upgraded to an "honorable discharge" and receive access to the VA and other resources. But it can be a very cumbersome process.

Danny has an elderly friend, who happens to be an African American woman. We were driving to an event, and she told the same story about younger people not understanding what we had to go through to get them where we are today. LGBTQ people are twice as likely to be sexually assaulted than other people. That is a very important issue. Discrimination. Now, in America, we all hold the military up. Americans respect the military more than any branch in government, but glaring prejudices are still being worked out. The Trump era flat out banned transgender people from serving in the military, whereas under President Joe Biden, effective April 30, 2021, several provisions activated:

- The military will provide service members a process by to transition gender while serving.
- A service member may not be involuntarily discharged or denied reenlistment solely on the basis of gender identity.
- Procedures will be developed for changing a service member's gender marker.
- The Defense Health Agency will develop clinical practice

guidelines to support the medical treatment of service members diagnosed with gender dysphoria.

With President Biden having signed an executive order repealing Trump's overtly discriminatory ban within his first week of office, ordering the secretary of defense and the secretary of homeland security to allow transgender servicemembers to serve openly, and these provisions, the military is now aligned with the freedoms it fights for.

CHAPTER 19
ACTIVISM ENSHRINED

ACTIVISM AND ADVOCACY is a wild ride in the United States where democracy reigns. Believe me, I'll never forget standing next to President Barack Obama when he signed the repeal of Don't Ask, Don't Tell into law. Depending on how our leaders are, as you see even between the time that I served in the military to now, in 2021, moral climate is either positive or negative. It is as definitive as the temperature outside! It affects all Americans and the world. I am one person, one man, and I want my story to be inspirational. I want my story to move something big forward. I don't want to put other people down in the process. I want to help. And as you now know, I want to serve.

I recognize my willpower to let negative vibes go though and not challenge people every time. It feels good when you don't give in every time and choose to sit back in neutral mode. Some people, like an old friend on Facebook, will say they don't want transgender in the military—try telling that to Kristin Beck, who is both a transgender person and a Navy Seal! I blocked him after thirty years of friendship since high school. I have no other way of contacting him. It's sad. I made that choice.

There are people I served with in the military who I've cut ties with. One said that everyone who got kicked out of the military for being gay simply needed to "stay put" and we couldn't go back and change their discharge. When I disagreed, he said, "So everyone we kicked out for marijuana, we should change their discharge, too?"

I said, "Those people made a choice."

He replied, "But gay people also chose to be gay." I couldn't even go further in the conversation, so there went the friendship. So, I chose to be gay, went to the military, hid who I was, all on purpose? In my talks, I reference different layers of intolerance and that we have lost a lot of civility in our society.

I have extremely strong willpower and determination. If I feel like I'm getting depressed, like now, I'm sitting here without my prosthetic because I hurt my hip yesterday, but I took the day off to relax my body. I'm not trying to be a superhero. I do have my limitations and I know when I need to recover. My recovery process is fast. Even when we lost the 2016 U.S. Presidential Election or sitting at the table with our tablets on social media, as soon as I feel down, I go outside by the pool and listen to the birds and the trees blowing. I escape scenarios that will put me in a state of unhappiness. I also talk to my role models, like Joe Solmonese. Sometimes I'm just asking for it though because he talks truth… always! Given the extensive work he's done and devotion he's had toward these causes in which lives like mine have substantially improved, he will do everything to prevent the clock from turning back. We remember that at one time, LGBTQ people were considered a disruption to national security because they are "promiscuous." "Reckless." "Loveless." They would "rape straight people of the same sex."

At one point after being injured, I wanted to stay in the Marines. I would still give my life for this country. So would my father. He insists, "When I see people in uniform, which is common in San Antonio, I remember wearing that uniform. I had burned it because of what I saw in Vietnam. People I golf with come to me and applaud me for being Eric's father."

There is potential for substantive backlash. People say they will never overturn marriage equality because it's too popular now, but maybe they will hear a series of cases that will change the law. They won't overturn Roe v. Wade but decide on cases that will make abortion inaccessible. (I hate to acknowledge that as of this writing, Texas has enacted a ban of abortion at six weeks of gestation, cementing my point.)

Joe adds: "When I went to San Antonio and told Eric to tell me his story, he went all the way back and then the story of his accident and then coming home. I was in tears. I was on the edge of my seat. I did not move for two hours listening to him. It's such an inspiring story. His activism, his decision to get involved. The repeal of Don't Ask, Don't Tell was incredibly inspiring. Eric has gone beyond activism and public service in a way that has the kind of outcome that most people only dream of! It's a big leap into a spotlight and a purpose and a mission. With Judy Shepherd, for eleven years, she did nothing but work to pass the Matthew Shepherd Hate Crimes Bill. I was with her the day this passed into law. How you move beyond and how your life is different depends on where you put that energy. In some ways, it's parallel to the movement. How has it changed after marriage and these big landmark things we got done?"

I answer this question every day by living the best that I can. Teaching at a university, I'm also in touch with younger people every day.

We are all a witness of several different generations crisscrossing the ether. I was part of a nonprofit group started by a mom of a girl who was bisexual and had no one to interact with. It's a group for teenagers, ages 12 to 15, who identify as LGBTQ. A young gentleman, 13, would go to school in a dress. I was so fearful for him.

I went to a conference in 2015 to accept an award. The conference had different sessions, with one being the guidelines for getting your military discharge overturned. About twelve people over forty attended. After the session, when these people were going down the stairs, much younger military people were coming up the stairs with Nordstrom Rack and Abercrombie bags. They had gone shopping. None of them thought of attending this session. DADT didn't touch them. They didn't want to be informed of the history. But I say, if you don't arm yourself with knowledge, history will repeat itself! Don't get too comfortable. I had asked someone in this age range if they knew who Harvey Milk was. He did not.

When I rolled my eyes, he replied, "Should I care?"

I voted at the age of seventeen. I was an honor student in government. I make it a point to tell young people this. I also donate my payment from speeches often. My payday is seeing youth inspired. I see a lot of tears, too, but I don't want them to feel sorry for my losing a leg. I want them to be purveyors of change. I don't know how much time I have left. I long to see that resonance on their faces—that which tells me they will look out for their brothers and sisters.

When my ex, Darrell, encouraged me to get on the battlefield of change, I knew that he didn't have to take that risk. We could have lived quietly. Who knows what would have transpired. I believe DADT may have ultimately been repealed, but my story solidified it.

Darrell is a psychotherapist with a private practice. In 2007, he was getting LGBTQ youth that were not out to parents because they weren't supportive. This has changed drastically, and Darrell gets parents who want to go to any length to make sure their children are happy. Parents talk to me about their struggles, too. Their future is brighter. They don't have to be afraid. In our generation, we didn't come out in high school or even as adults oftentimes. We pretended to be college roommates. They don't have to hide hopefully. Those doors have been kicked open. Transgender people, however, have the highest murder rate of a minority group in the United States. We've made tremendous progress, but kids are coming out much earlier. They don't have to be looked at as a special group but just as people, as Americans.

After retiring from my career in the Marines, you should know that my friendships with Mike, Carlos, Brian, Lavon, Nicholas, and others only strengthened. Experiencing a life-or-death situation in war with these men was profound. The very nature of Marines is loyalty. The very nature of my birth name, Fidelis, is faithful. I may have exchanged this name in the public sphere, but I embrace what it means. In the end, my entire story is about brotherhood, sisterhood...community—finding it, nurturing it, and protecting it with my life.

REFERENCES

Interviews by the Author

Brian Alaniz. Phone interview. November 18, 2018.

Fidelis Alva. In-person interview. September 14, 2018.

Lois Alva. In-person interview. September 14, 2018.

Roger Gomez. Phone interview. August 17, 2018.

Nicholas Hengtes. Phone interview. September 4, 2018.

Carlos Huerta. Phone interview. November 12, 2018.

Danny Ingram. In-person interview. September 13, 2018.

Mike Kaniuk. Phone interview. August 13, 2018.

Brian Lafferty. Phone interview. September 4, 2018.

Darrell Parsons. Phone interview. December 6, 2018.

Lavon Peters. Phone interview. September 5, 2018.

Joe Solmonese. Phone interview. September 5, 2018.

Publications

Alva, Eric. "Op-Ed: Gay Purple Heart Recipient Says 'Mission Not Accomplished.'" *Advocate*. May 25, 2015. https://www.advocate.com/commentary/2015/05/25/op-ed-gay-purple-heart-recipient-says-mission-not-accomplished

Blakemore, Erin. "The Revolutionary War Hero Who Was Openly Gay." History. June 12, 2019. https://www.history.com/news/openly-gay-revolutionary-war-hero-friedrich-von-steuben

C-Span. "Gays and Lesbians in the Military." July 23, 2008. https://www.c-span.org/video/?206528-1/gays-lesbians-military

College of Charleston. "On Veteran's Day, Dr. James Ficke Talks About Being a Soldier and Surgeon." *The College Today*. November 7, 2014.

https://today.cofc.edu/2014/11/07/
veterans-day-dr-james-ficke-talks-soldier-surgeon/
Human Rights Campaign. "Eric Alva on Don't Ask Don't Tell."
September 21, 2010. Youtube.com.
https://www.youtube.com/watch?v=b8oy1yF4Qf4
Jarvis, Jamie. "Ex-Marine Eric Alva speaks to commemorate
National Coming Out Day." *The Globe Online*. October
19, 2011. http://www.globeslcc.com/2011/10/19/
ex-marine-eric-alva-speaks-to-commemorate-national-
coming-out-day/
LGBT History Month. Eric Alva.
https://lgbthistorymonth.com/eric-alva?tab=biography
Miller, James. "Marine Vets Fight for Equality." *The Mesquite*.
October 17, 2017.
https://mesquite-news.com/marine-vet-fights-for-equality/
Mitchell, Robert. "Gay Marine Helps Change History." *The
Harvard Gazette*. April 7, 2017.
https://news.harvard.edu/gazette/story/2017/04/eric-alva-
shares-story-of-being-gay-a-marine-and-changing-history/
Rose, Rex. "Q & A with Eric Alva." *The East Carolinian*.
October 12, 2012.
http://www.theeastcarolinian.com/lifestyles/article_b2a57dc6-
4550-5a17-bd7c-16176048b3e6.html
Vargas, Jose Antonio. "Defending His Country, but Not
Its 'Don't Ask, Don't Tell' Policy." *The Washington Post*.
February 28, 2007.
https://www.washingtonpost.com/wp-dyn/content/
article/2007/02/27/AR2007022701589.html
Veterans Coming Home. "Coming Home San Antonio | Eric
Alva."
http://veteranscominghome.org/station_media/
coming-home-san-antonio-eric-alva-2/

9 781737 553007